MOMENTS

of

GLAD
GRACE

a memoir

Alison Wearing

Published by ECW Press
665 Gerrard Street East
Toronto, Ontario, Canada M4M 1Y2
416-694-3348 / info@ecwpress.com

Get the
eBook free!*
*proof of purchase
required

Editor for the Press: Susan Renouf
Cover design: David A. Gee
Cover image: "Dublin Pub" © Charles Hewitt / Stringer /
Getty Images International
Author photo: © Mark Raynes Roberts

To the best of her abilities, the author has related experiences,
places, people, and organizations from her memories of them.
In order to protect the privacy of others, she has, in some
instances, changed the names of certain people and details of
events and places.

Purchase the print edition
and receive the eBook free.
For details, go to ecwpress.com/eBook.

LIBRARY AND ARCHIVES CANADA CATALOGUING IN
PUBLICATION

Title: Moments of glad grace : a memoir / Alison
Wearing.

Names: Wearing, Alison, 1967– author.

Identifiers: Canadiana (print) 20190218606
Canadiana (ebook) 20190218630

ISBN 978-1-77041-513-3 (softcover)
ISBN 978-1-77305-498-8 (PDF)
ISBN 978-1-77305-497-1 (EPUB)

Subjects: LCSH: Wearing, Alison, 1967– | LCSH:
Wearing, Alison, 1967—Family. | LCSH: Fathers and
daughters—Canada. | LCGFT: Autobiographies.

Classification: LCC HQ755.85 .W43 2020
DDC 306.874/2—dc23

The publication of *Moments of Glad Grace* has been generously supported by the Canada Council for the Arts which last
year invested $153 million to bring the arts to Canadians throughout the country and is funded in part by the Government
of Canada. *Nous remercions le Conseil des arts du Canada de son soutien. L'an dernier, le Conseil a investi 153 millions de dollars pour
mettre de l'art dans la vie des Canadiennes et des Canadiens de tout le pays. Ce livre est financé en partie par le gouvernement du Canada.*
We acknowledge the support of the Ontario Arts Council (OAC), an agency of the Government of Ontario, which last year
funded 1,737 individual artists and 1,095 organizations in 223 communities across Ontario for a total of $52.1 million. We also
acknowledge the contribution of the Government of Ontario through the Ontario Book Publishing Tax Credit, and through
Ontario Creates for the marketing of this book.

PRINTED AND BOUND IN CANADA

PRINTING: FRIESENS   5   4   3   2   1

MIX
Paper from
responsible sources
FSC® C016245

Praise for *Confessions of a Fairy's Daughter*

"*Confessions of a Fairy's Daughter* had me in tears: first of laughter, then of sadness, then of wonder at life's strange and marvelous fragility. It is a book both beautiful and true; about the longing for family and for home. Alison Wearing is a hugely talented writer."
— ALISON PICK, author of the Man Booker Prize–nominated *Far to Go*

"This exquisitely written and deeply compassionate memoir tells the story of a family and a nation at a turning point in their sexual and political awakening . . . This book is for anyone who chooses to live (and love) openly and freely."
— KAMAL AL-SOLAYLEE, author of *Intolerable* and *Brown*

"Part memoir, part history book, part diary and all parts heart. Alison Wearing weaves a tale that celebrates the complexities of who we are and the families we hold close. *Confessions of a Fairy's Daughter* is painful, tender, poignant and — most important — beautifully honest."
— BRIAN FRANCIS, author of *Break in Case of Emergency* and *Fruit*

Praise for *Honeymoon in Purdah*

"One of the best pieces of travel writing it has been my privilege to read in this, or any, millennium." — *Ottawa Citizen*

"As with any good travel book, *Honeymoon in Purdah* is not a tour of monuments, but an exploration of a nation's psyche, in this case a proud, generous, and enduring one." — *Globe and Mail*

"Bright and searingly observant, [Wearing] paints indelible moments from her honeymoon with Iran . . . The cumulative effect is like reading *Alice in Wonderland*." — *Toronto Star*

"This book is why we travel and why we read travel writing: to be transported, and to return transformed." — JAMIE ZEPPA, author of *Beyond the Sky and the Earth: A Journey Into Bhutan*

For my family,
both blood & soul.

AUTHOR'S NOTE

It seems only fair to offer anonymity to people who find themselves as characters in books. For no matter how hard writers might try to be accurate in our portrayals, the people we paint onto the pages of memoir are only ever characters inspired by real people, renditions that almost invariably differ from how those same individuals see themselves.

To some in this book I have offered the simple mask of a pseudonym, to others a slightly more elaborate costume: a wig, a change of birthplace or spouse. Sticklers might say that such smudges to the canvas are only permissible in the galleries of fiction, but rather than hampering the truth of a portrait, I believe these brushstrokes are sometimes necessary for it to freely emerge.

The one person who cannot be disguised is my father. I was as surprised as anyone to find myself writing yet another memoir that cast him as a central figure, but he has been gracious and generous in his understanding that inspiration is a mysterious energy, writing evolves with its own inner dynamics, and, in the end, books are as much crafted by the writer as they are birthed.

When you are old and grey and full of sleep,
And nodding by the fire, take down this book,
And slowly read, and dream of the soft look
Your eyes had once, and of their shadows deep;

How many loved your moments of glad grace,
And loved your beauty with love false or true,
But one man loved the pilgrim soul in you,
And loved the sorrows of your changing face.

— W.B. YEATS

SATURDAY

DUBLIN AIRPORT

The customs officer has the face of a merry alcoholic who also enjoys his pie. His friendly eyes flutter when I tell him the purpose of my trip — to help my father with some gynaecological research — but he doesn't ask any further questions. Just stamps my passport and says, *Welcome to Ireland, love,* which feels like a moment of sanity in an otherwise crazed world.

I have come here to help my father with some genealogical research. He's quite serious about it and has been at it for years, but a few months ago he mentioned a desire to revisit Dublin's libraries and archives, adding that he would prefer to do it with the help of a research assistant. *Count me in!* I'd said immediately, though we both know I fall asleep at the mere mention of genealogy, a word I am forever confusing with gynaecology, particularly when saying it aloud.

Still, we're here. And a bit of boredom in the archives seems a small price to pay for the chance to spend ten days in Dublin with my dad. He'll be eighty in a few months — he'd say he's seventy-nine and a half — and is so fit and active I have wondered if I'll be the one scrambling to keep up. But he also has incipient Parkinson's, a disease that has begun to possess and hammer him, and I jumped at a chance for time together now.

My father does not appear in the collage of tired faces watching a slow parade of suitcases file past. We weren't sitting together on the plane, having bought our tickets separately, and I didn't see him in any of the lines at customs. I park myself in a visible spot and pass the time by trying to conjure a border experience which includes the phrase *Welcome to the United States of America, love,* but no matter how many times I attempt to lift that small kite of words into being, I am unable to keep it aloft.

When most of the bags are claimed from the belt and there is still no sign of him, I notice that when a parent is about to turn eighty, a child's reflex changes from *Where the hell's he gone?* to *What if something's happened?* I walk and peer and swivel and conclude that he must have headed out of the arrivals area without me. And, indeed, on the other side of the exit's automatic doors, I spot him looking bored. The moment I wave, however, he becomes animated, fluttering a hand to his chest and panting in theatrical, exaggerated relief while running through a breathless explanation: *I didn't see you in there so I came out here but then I realized you must have been back there but then I wasn't allowed back in so I just had to stand here wondering how long you'd stay there waiting for me!* He is giggling now, shedding so many layers of relief and excitement that I pause to wonder if the airport cleaning staff ever feel they are mopping up excess emotion in addition to casual grime. Relieved, my dad goes off to find the toilets while I stand guard over the suitcases. As I watch him disappear, I decide to begin our father-daughter escapade by creating a running list of qualities I adore about him, flipping to the back of my notebook and creating the heading *Things about Dad,* before printing *How Often He Giggles.*

A few minutes later, I look up to see him scurrying back to where I am waiting with the bags — he is not a plodder, my father; he has two speeds: Resting and Scurrying — and despite the speed at which his legs are swishing and padding along the shiny airport floor, I have time to add *And the Way He Scurries* before flipping my notebook shut.

~

This is my first time in Ireland. I've always intended to come, but other sunnier, more exotic places always seemed to win out. Now that I'm here, though, I can't believe how long it's taken me to arrive. I feel giddy, springy, can't wait to get out and explore the city, the pubs, the famously green countryside, to fill my ears with jocular idioms, to lap up everything there is to lap. Our taxi driver is kind and talkative, effervescent with stories of weather, both typical and atypical, and the type of clothing he generally wears both winter and summer. I am delighted by his accent to a clichéd degree. He offers to take us *sru de parrk* on our way to our destination and I am so seduced that I tell him that would be a splendid idea, having never said *splendid idea* in my life and sounding ridiculous as I do so. The driver exits the highway, amps up his chattiness a few more notches, and drives a long arc through an unremarkable expanse of grass and trees while cheerfully doubling his fare.

But who cares, we're in Ireland! On our way to an Airbnb, as about 75 percent of his customers are doing these days, the driver tells us. My dad booked the place a few months ago and while I wasn't sure about it from the photos — I'm afraid there might be a black-and-white cow skin on the living room floor — I've found that few of these places actually resemble their photos, so we might be pleasantly surprised.

"Oh, dat's a luvely area," the driver assures us with a nice round *u* in *luvely*, adding that he believes we'll be very happy there indeed.

He winds through a series of narrow cobblestone streets into a quaint, historic neighbourhood and leaves us at the front gates of the old Jameson Distillery. Which is odd, until we learn that the polished limestone building was recently remodelled to house a whiskey museum and a cluster of condos holding the echoes of three centuries of people saying *cheers*.

Indeed, I believe we'll be very happy here.

10 BOW STREET

The apartment is bright and spacious with a clever triangular addition to the main room made of floor-to-ceiling windows, the ideal renovation in a country not known for excessive sunlight. What looked in the photos like a black-and-white cow skin on the living room floor is, in fact, a black-and-white cow skin on the living room floor, but I silently name it Stephen Harper, which helps. Our landlord, or host, or whatever he's called, John, does not smile as he shows us around, but he is immensely kind and sorry for everything: the fact that the plumbing is antiquated, the water only heats up twice a day, the wash machine's sluggish, the economy's a disaster, and there's no government, but there is a good fish shop around the corner, and if we like, he can show us around.

I like John.

Before we go out, my dad asks about the political situation and if there is any sign of a government being formed soon. I join the conversation by nodding, though I have no idea what they are talking about, being both ignorant of Irish politics (obviously) and shamelessly unprepared for this trip. I don't know why, but I didn't read a word about Ireland before I left, save a book of fairy tales by W.B. Yeats and James Joyce's *Dubliners*, which I started on the plane.

John's head falls back at the mention of politics and he lets it hang there a few moments before lifting it and speaking.

"Here it is, right here," he says, jamming a finger at a small white box mounted on the wall. "People are more than stretched as it is, out of work and bleedin' themselves to the banks, and then we're told we have to start *payin' for water*." He slows down as he intones those last three words. "And then they start installin' *these things*," he sneers, giving the water meter a hard flick with his fingers on the words *dese tings*. "And the people just up and refused to pay. That's what brought the government down. And they'll not be gettin' up as far as I can see. It's a mess, I tell you. A *mess*."

He throws up his hands before opening the apartment door. "After you," he says and holds out his arm, though the hallway is so narrow there is barely enough room to get past.

My dad asks John a few more questions about the various political parties that might form a coalition government. I don't follow John's mumbled answers to that (something about incompetence and *bloody eejits*), but my dad responds by asking about Ireland's economy, the effects of the devastating crash, and whether the slight upturn that has been reported recently is noticeable yet.

The moment we're outside, John lights up a cigarette and takes a long, patient drag.

"Well, it was lunacy before the crash, I'll give you that. Commerce absolutely *exploded*, buildings goin' up faster than a guy could piss, banks loanin' money to any muppet with a pulse. All of a sudden, the people had money. *Loads* of it. You never saw anythin' like it before. Lads buyin' houses like it was rounds at the pub, spendin' money like it was a race to get rid of it. It was mad as a box of frogs."

He tsks the memory, then rolls his eyes so dramatically they nearly tumble off his face.

"And you know about the crash in 2008," he says. *De crash in too tousand an eight.* "Well, you might know of it, but you can't imagine it, the numbers of people turned out of their homes, out of work, homeless. It was *deadly*. You hear about a property bubble burstin', but it's millions of people's hearts that burst. Diabolical. We lost everythin'. And the *debt*," he says, with an airy clip on the final *t*. "Figures the mind can't even begin to comprehend."

He pauses, takes a long drag on his cigarette, squints up at the tops of buildings.

"The Irish people's gonna spend the next seventy-five or one hundred years payin' off that debt. Not the banks who were tossin' it out like candy, mind you, the Irish *people*. And it's not like we did anythin' wrong. We just *worked*, for chrissakes, but it's like Ireland's just come out of a war. And *lost*."

He takes a quick puff and yanks out his cigarette.

"And then the IMF and the EU forced our heads into a bucket of austerity shite and I'll tell you what they shoulda called it: Ireland's Treaty of Versailles. Cuts everywhere, no jobs. It's been the worst damn time Ireland's had since the Great Hunger. We might be startin' to pull out of the worst of it, I'll give you that, but it's only 'cause America and Britain's bounced back and we're exportin' again, not 'cause the Irish people's sufferin' paid off."

John exhales a long plume of smoke before guiding us through an alleyway at the back of the distillery. We emerge in a large public square, a cobblestone pedestrian area lined with shops and restaurants. It's attractive and welcoming, clearly in the process of gentrification, though not in an overly boutiquey way, at least not yet. For the time being, it feels balanced, with blocks of spartan working-class townhouses on one side of the long plaza, and cafés, restaurants, and a grocery store on the other.

John gives us a quick history of the neighbourhood, Smithfield, noting that even a few years ago it was still pretty dodgy but it's now on the up and up. They're even planning to relocate one of the big colleges here, along with housing for thousands of students. *Tousands of 'em.*

"You'll find the fish shop on the other side," John tells us, pointing to a block of tenement housing. "Everything's fresh every day, o' course. And then over here's a café, nice place, coffee's grand, and there's newspapers, even wifi. There's a couple of other cafés along here too, but Turd Space is the best," he says, gesturing at the window as we walk past.

I glance up at the sign — *Third Space Café* — and turn to my dad, who winks and smiles. At the end of the square is a pub that looks grotty from the outside, but John assures us it's a wonderful spot.

"Live music every night and not the tourist shite you'll find in Temple Bar. Here's the real thing, just local people bringin' their instruments. It's mighty."

John guides us to the neighbourhood grocery store and goes so far as to tour us through some of the aisles, pointing out the prepared meals he can recommend at the butcher's counter, the corner where the wine can be found, the various beers we'll want to try, the local cheeses. As we're leaving the shop, a young woman approaches us asking for money for *de Lewis* and John reaches into his pocket and puts several coins in her hand.

"You get a lot of that around here," he tells us quietly once she's thanked him and moved away. "But what are people supposed to do without work? The economy's in bits. Here," he says, pointing to the other end of the square, "I'll just show you where you can catch the Lewis she was talkin' about."

The *Luas*, as it turns out, is the local tram and there is a stop a short spit from our building.

"It'll take you right across town above ground. It's grand. Or the river's right there and you have a lovely walk to town, shouldn't take you more than twenty minutes," he says, quickly scanning my father, assessing his fitness.

And it's at that moment I realize that we're turfing John out of his own flat. Of course we are. I feel a hollowing in my chest, a combination of guilt and immediate attempts to mitigate same with comforting thoughts of the *but he must be happy for the income* variety, none of which help.

John leaves us at the entrance of the distillery and wishes us a wonderful stay, gives us his cell number, and asks us to let him know if we have any problems.

"And best of luck findin' the ancestors!" he says, shaking our hands and smiling for the first time.

We thank him for his help and drag our jetlagged jelly-legs back up to the apartment, where we spend five minutes being audibly relieved at how nice the place is, John, the neighbourhood, before — zonk — performing face plants into our pillows.

An hour or so later, my dad knocks softly at my door.

"It's eleven a.m.," he says quietly. "We should probably get up now if we want to adjust to local time."

I lift the polished round limestone that is apparently my head and say "good idea," before crashing back onto my pillow. A few minutes later, I hear him scurrying back down the hallway towards my room. I am just about to shout "I'M UP! I'M UP!" when he apologizes and asks if I can help him make a pot of coffee. Something's happened.

I can hear the wrinkling in his voice, a crackling that's crept in recently. Most of the time I don't notice it, or I ignore it, but as I lie here bulldozed by exhaustion, with my eyes closed and my guard down, I cannot help but hear the rocky bed beneath the river of his voice. And how shallow that water has begun to sound.

TURD SPACE CAFÉ

We gave up trying to make coffee and came here instead. John has one of those stainless steel espresso makers that heats up on the stove and while it's a simple enough contraption, my dad had never used one before. It can be fiddly twisting it apart, figuring out how much water and coffee to put in so that it boils up properly (every pot seems to have its quirks), but the main problem was that my dad's arm kept shaking while he was twisting it all together, and somewhere in the shuffle, the entire package of coffee grounds ended up spilling all over the floor.

He was good-natured about it, mildly frustrated, perhaps, but only briefly, suggesting we go out for breakfast instead. *We could try the Turd Space Café!* he said cheerfully. And after spreading the coffee grounds around the kitchen with a broom as effective as a giant paintbrush, we did.

We have.

And John was right: the coffee's great. And it's a good place for newspapers. We are both buried in them as we sip and chew and try to wake up before deciding how to spend our first Dublin day. My dad nestles around his newspaper covetously, almost predatorily, like a carnivorous plant curling around a dead bug, newsprint being as essential a nutritional component of his breakfast as coffee and toast. The newspaper is swishing and rustling loudly across the table as he turns the pages with a quaking hand. I watch it out of the corner of my eye, then I look away, because it's easier, less heartbreaking, and because I don't want him to notice me noticing.

I grab the *Irish Times* and do a quick read-up on the situation with the government — namely, why there isn't one — and learn that since a vote of no confidence that brought the government down more than eight weeks ago, the country's been left with a hung parliament, and more than 70 percent of those elected have no wish to be in power. Seems it's easier to be in opposition until this whole water meter crisis blows over; or perhaps it's the whole economic crisis the parliamentarians are waiting to blow over. (According to John, seventy-five years ought to do it.) Either way, no one appears to want to be in charge, a situation I'm not sure I've ever run into before.

I log onto the café's wifi to look up Ireland's debt and connect to the National Debt Clock, a website which offers the figures in "a clear and friendly way so that everybody can understand." According to this site, the Irish national debt is about 200 billion euros (about $289 billion or $64,000 per person — more than twice Canada's per capita debt), but, like the seconds on a digital clock, the numbers are constantly changing, going up by about 300 euros per second. In the few moments I've been on the site, in fact, the Irish National Debt has risen, in a clear and friendly way, by tens of thousands of euros. Watching the numbers flip and increase so quickly makes me jittery, so I scroll down to see what other information I can find.

Under the heading *Interesting Facts* are the following thoughts and exclamation marks:

You could wrap one euro bills around the Earth 896 times with the debt amount!

If you lay the debt amount in one euro bills on top of each other, they would make a pile 25,149 kilometres high! That's equivalent to 0.07 trips to the Moon!

I relay these statistics to my dad, who is too focused on his newspaper to hear what I am saying. The U.S. primaries are in full swing and my dad, a retired political science professor, says following them feels like gawking at a train wreck, but he can't help himself.

"Just when you think the Republican party can't get any more pathetic, they get even more pathetic! *WUUUUUH!*"

That last word is his trademark shriek. It is the sound of someone getting goosed. The sound a human voice would make if there were a slide whistle attached to it. The sound vocal cords might make if they were shaken out and snapped like a wet towel. In my father's case, it is a protean sound, capable of conveying surprise, horror, delight, or distress. He utters it as he has always uttered it: as if he were in a soundproof pod.

Which we are not. We are in a café. So the moment after the shriek has sounded — *WUUUUUH!* — every single person turns to face us. My dad is wholly unaware of the attention. He turns the page and begins reading something else, while I raise my eyebrows and smile around the room trying to convey reassurance.

It is a practised look. I've donned it throughout my life. But only today do I notice that the very things that might once have driven us bonkers about a parent can, over time, become sources of endearment. I flip to the back of my notebook and write *That Outrageous WUUUUUH! Sound* before pausing with my pen in my mouth to come up with something for a column I have created on the opposite side of the page: *Smart Business Ideas*. The column is there not because I am smart or businessy, but because I am the opposite and weary of penury. The only entry I have so far is *Open a Tattoo Removal Clinic*. To that I add, *Buy Real Estate in Dublin before Economy Fully Recovers*. But then I think of John, and of all the people I'd be trying to sell it to at a profit, people who are already bleeding to the banks, and I cross out the whole sentence. Also, less altruistically, I can't afford to buy real estate in Dublin, or anywhere else.

∽

My dad is wrestling with his newspaper now. It swishes and rustles across the table as he tries to turn the pages. His left hand has a life of its own, literally, as if it housed a demanding presence that is forever grabbing and tugging him.

It was the swim coach who first pointed it out a few years ago, when my dad was still with a swim club at the University of Toronto, practising with them a couple of times a week. Being in his seventies, he was (by far) the oldest one in the club, and while I found it impressive that he was swimming as much as he was, he was also presented with the Most Likely to Be Chatting at the End of the Lane award at one of the club's famously fun Christmas parties, so I don't think it unfair to say that the practices were as much a social event for my dad as an athletic one.

"Joe, your hand is shaking," the coach said after one of the practices. My dad looked down. To his surprise, it was true. But he felt fine. Normal. Rode home on his bicycle. Showed his partner. Went to the doctor, did a series of tests, was told he'd probably had a mild stroke, that the shaking might fade over time, and that it was definitely not Parkinson's. Which came as a thunderous relief.

The shaking didn't fade. And a couple of years later, a new doctor did another series of tests and told him that it definitely was Parkinson's, albeit a slow-progressing version. Whatever that means.

"What does that mean again?" I ask over the newspapers.

My dad shrugs. Isn't sure. Isn't sure his doctor knows either. "But every few months, I have to go back and do a bunch of tests." He looks down at the newspaper, then up again, brightening. "One of them is counting backwards from a hundred by intervals of seven. Try it!"

"93 . . . 86 . . . 79 . . ." I start.

"Yes, but I've found a way to cheat!" he announces. "You go down ten and add three. That's much easier than subtracting seven."

I start again. "100, 93, 86, 79 . . . wait . . ."

"Yes, you have to be careful!"

"79, 72, 65, 58 . . . 51 . . ."

"That's right . . ."

"44, 37, 30, 23, 16, 9, 2."

"Yes, that's it. You've done it correctly if you end on two. Isn't that clever?"

"Yeah." I smile. Drain my coffee cup. "But wait, is it clever to cheat on a medical test?"

My dad shrugs. "I wish I could cheat on all the tests." Returns to his newspaper.

I am about to return to mine, but instead, I take a moment to conduct a small ritual: the encircling of moments I wish to remember, moments I recognize as precious, ephemeral, worth gathering into an invisible mental archive, a psychic photograph album of sorts. The day my son created an oatmeal mural on the kitchen table with such boundless, limb-flexing, cackle-thick joy I wasn't sure he would ever stop laughing; the sight of my mother's sleeping face at dawn the day I realized she'd become an older woman, no longer the person — inexhaustible, capable of anything, available for everyone — I had held static until then; the view of my partner standing on the shore of Lake Huron in the wind with his arms outstretched, our son toddling up behind him and mimicking the posture, two creatures drying their wings together, baring their chests to the sky.

And this moment, here, in the Turd Space Café, not because there is anything particularly special about this scene — *I wish I could cheat on all the tests* — but because I know how easy it is to rush to the next distraction, hurtle carelessly past beauty, let life barrel past. I've done that for too much of my life: run ahead, kept one eye on the lookout for something more exciting, been so trained on future possibilities that I miss what is lying, peacefully and exquisitely, in front of me. And I don't want to do that anymore. I don't want take anything for granted, not even this small moment. I want to appreciate it all.

∽

This is our first trip together, just the two of us, unless you count the time we spent a few days in Paris together thirty years ago, when I was a teenager traipsing through Europe in search of myself and my dad was at the end of an opera binge. By the time we met up at the Gare de l'Est, I had been on my own for six months and was deep into a project of reinvention that had involved shearing my head (on one side only), speaking with a bizarre accent of no traceable origin, and wearing long, flowing scarves that were forever either tripping or strangling me. My plan had been to step off the train Transformed and Together. Which worked, until I spotted my dad galloping the length of the platform, waving so excitedly that I thought his arm might detach and go hurtling across the station. *I LOVE THE HAIRDO!* he called, practically toppling over himself to get to me faster. The sight of him squelched all my efforts at sophistication and I relaxed back into my ragged, messy self, where I stayed for the rest of our time together.

Once we'd untangled ourselves from the train station, we checked into a once opulent, now dilapidated *pension* near the Jardin du Luxembourg. I remember feeling the floral curtains and wobbly glass doorknobs before washing my undies in the sink and draping them, dripping, over everything. As I recall, my dad got annoyed and scurried around behind me, picking up panties as if they were the tails of dead mice, relocating them to the radiators one by one, and scolding me for not respecting the furniture. But after that, we got on famously. Ate, drank, and wandered for days, father and daughter on a lark.

The hotel policy was to leave breakfast on a tray outside the room, so every morning we would lounge in our pyjamas for hours, licking greasy croissant flakes from our fingertips, sipping milky lukewarm coffee, and discussing the mysteries of sex and sexuality.

It wasn't typical father-daughter talk perhaps, but we were coming through an atypical time. My dad had come out of the closet five years earlier, he and my mother had divorced, and I had a new stepfather, four stepsiblings, and a fairy stepmother named Michael. My dad and I had talked about things as they were happening, of course, but there was something about being together in that elegant, faraway room, surrounded by foreign words and drying undies, that opened an intimacy we hadn't found until then.

I asked the questions I had never asked before. He answered everything with an honesty that felt brutal at times but was generous, in the way that truth is. We both, as I remember it, wept. And then at last we got dressed and went out and linked arms and marvelled at the petrified music that is architecture, the sculpted love that is family, and at how being together like that made life seem possible again, manageable for a moment, rife with plausible beauty.

Thirty years later, when my dad invited me to travel with him to Ireland, I had imagined another sojourn like that Paris one, I suppose, though blessedly less littered with the shrapnel of divorce and shame. We're both fairly settled in life and self these days, in as much as anyone ever is. He'll soon be eighty and is still game for adventure, and I'm on the precipice of a half-century of living, in full knowledge of how precious this is, the time we have with people we love, this blink of time on Earth, this time in Ireland with my dad.

~∽

"Okay!" he says cheerfully, closing the paper and straightening up. "Let's wander around and get lost and see what we find!"

After a quick joke involving our nickname for this café, I go off to find the toilet. When I return, my dad is standing at the till paying for our breakfasts. That's the arrangement — he's covering food and lodging in exchange for my research assistance — but watching him pick up the tab, as he has done virtually all my life, has an instantly infantilizing effect. By the time I join him at the counter, I am twelve years old. He is about to put his wallet away when he opens it again and passes me a fifty euro bill.

"Why don't you take this?"

I laugh. "Why?"

"Well, just some spending money."

I laugh again, awkwardly now. "It's okay, I don't need spending money. I mean, I have spending money, I have *money* . . ."

Neither one of us acknowledges that this is, kind of, a lie. I've just endured a killer year with two large gigs falling through at the last minute, one only days after the other, followed by a series of large and unanticipated expenses, coupled with, how do I put this, three decades of life in the arts and not much in the way of gargantuan economic prospects on the horizon.

"Well, why don't you take it anyway," he says, dealing the bill casually like it's a bad playing card he's trying to discard. "I don't like to carry around too much cash."

I smile, sort of. Feel equal parts grateful and mortified. Tuck the bill in my pocket, feel briefly nauseous, and hurry out the door.

Where it's *sunny*. We are both actually squinting. The sky is a cerulean song. Which means, in a way, that this trip has already exceeded my expectations. I'm in a short wool coat with layers of cotton and wool beneath that, but it is balmy compared to the endless drizzle I'd been warned an Irish spring might have on daily offer.

After a few short blocks, we reach the riverbank and the water of the Liffey sparkles in such a way that it is impossible not to smile. My dad and I lean over the railing, inhaling our first long view of the city: the domes and spires, impressive Georgian buildings, bridges that arch over the water at regular intervals as far as we can see.

"Oh, Dad!" I say, threading my arm into his. "Look, we're in Dublin!"

My dad giggles and pulls me closer. "Yes, and isn't it *grand!*"

TRINITY COLLEGE

We've been walking for five hours. Five straight hours and it was my idea to sit down. My dad might be turning eighty and living with Parkinson's, but he's still in remarkably good shape, a fact that is not so much surprising as it is reassuring.

He's always been a fit and vital soul: cycling and walking all over Toronto as a proud non-owner of a car for more than thirty years, singing in choirs, practising the piano daily for hours at a time, swimming three times a week, and engaged with so many friends and dinner parties and concert series and travels that it is as difficult to make plans with him as it is with someone half his age. Still, I cannot remember the last time I spent a full day walking around with him, and I am relieved to see he still has it in him.

My dad's nephew, my cousin Robin, a former athlete nearly twenty years younger than my dad, received the same diagnosis at about the same time and Robin's body has already cemented, his face hardened, his gait now a trudge.

∽

The walk has been brilliant, the city fantastic, even the pubs in the Temple Bar neighbourhood classically charming, if blatantly touristy, as John warned. *Pubs: the official sunblock of Ireland* reads a sign in one of the pub windows.

The bench where I've suggested we stop and rest is on the grounds of Trinity College. It's a compact campus in the centre of the city, built around courtyards and leafy public squares, so the place feels spacious, luxuriant, peaceful. Our bench on the edge of the College Green offers a view of a dozen or so male students playing a barefoot game of soccer. They're juiced up with sunshine and youth, dancing light-footed around the ball, their joy effusive, contagious. The trees lining the green are laden with white blossoms that send down a dappled, scented shade, and it couldn't be a lovelier moment in a lovelier spot.

Always one to enjoy the view of fine specimens of the male body, my dad is admiring the scene as though it were a moving portrait of the finest art. "This is almost as good as going to a bathhouse," he muses dreamily. "That's another nice way to get over jet lag."

I turn and raise an eyebrow.

"Well, it is!" he says, rushing to his own defence. "One time when Michael and I travelled to Paris, we arrived so early in the morning that we had hours to kill before we were able to check into our hotel, so we were sitting in a train station because that was one of the few places open at that hour. And then I had a brainwave."

My father never has ideas, always brainwaves. These are far more exciting and worth having than mere ideas.

He sits up, enlivened. "I knew from a previous visit that there was a gay bathhouse in that area and of course the idea of spending the morning lounging in hot tubs and steam rooms with naked men was very appealing, so Michael stayed behind with the luggage and I went off to make sure it was open. And it was!" He lifts both arms in front of him — *ta-da!* — then crumples. "But just as I was leaving, the proprietor said, *Now you do understand that there are women here as well as men*" He sighs. "Well! We just couldn't wrap our minds around that!"

I can feel my face crinkling. "Wrap your minds around what?"

He shrugs, stirs the air with one hand. Stirs and stirs and stirs. "Well . . . the idea of . . . being around . . . naked women."

I open my mouth to respond, but no words rush for the door. It's not that I'm shocked. My dad's been out of the closet, exuberantly, for forty years. My mouth is open and empty of sound because he still says things that surprise me. And I'm about to say as much when two of the soccer players tackle a third and bodies begin tumbling all over each other, pouring laughter onto the grass.

"Oh, that looks like such fun," my dad says, his smile broad and warm.

We watch as the players untangle themselves, jump to their feet, slap each other on the back. They lather each other with playful assurances and the ball is kicked in a long, high arc to the far side of the field.

Time passes.

A breeze twirls blossoms from a branch.

"So, did you go?" I ask.

Pause.

"Did I go where?"

"You and Michael. To the bathhouse."

"No-no, no-no," he says, his voice bouncing rhythmically across the words. "We waited in the train station."

I puff out a laugh. "You opted to sit on a hard bench in a train station over steam rooms and saunas just because there might have been naked women there?"

My father sighs. Deeply. "Yes. Just thinking about it turned us both off the whole idea."

I take a breath, shake my head, and look back out at the game.

Watch a short sexy guy with a shock of dark hair fancy-foot his way
past the defence and score a goal.

Arms fly up around him. Cheers rake the sky.

"Well, Dad, I'd say that confirms it."

He is watching one of the players. Speaks distractedly. "Confirms
what?"

I lay my hand on his arm. "You're definitely gay."

He smiles. Doesn't take his eyes off the game. "Oh, good."

∼

A few minutes later, his head tilts back slightly and he is fast asleep.

He's always been able to do that: sleep anywhere. Even an hour
or so before giving a concert, he can lie down and sleep for twenty
minutes — just like that. While every other performer I know is
wound up like a top an hour before curtain, pacing, gnawing lips,
flicking fingers, waggling jaws, my dad (who has played the piano
all his life, but rededicated himself seriously after he retired and
now performs in small concerts with other amateur pianists) simply
reclines on the nearest available flat surface, closes his eyes, and
drifts off. He doesn't even set an alarm. He just sniffs himself awake
after about a quarter of an hour and sits upright, refreshed, as if
something marvellous has just occurred to him.

It has: a concert.

Half an hour later, he's playing Chopin.

I have never noticed before that his tremors stop when he sleeps.
As though the disease lies down and falls asleep alongside him, relaxing the grip it holds around him. He looks tranquil, relaxed, free,
and watching him rest so peacefully makes me long to steal him
away before it stirs. Tiptoe away and outrun the damn thing.

∼

We have an early dinner at a pub near John's flat. The beer menu is almost as long as *Ulysses* and is full of draft names like *Of Foam and Fury* and *Fuck Art the Heathens Are Coming*, both of which we order, along with food that is so forgettable it was clearly designed as chewy, absorbent material to facilitate the ordering of more beer. Within a few bland bites and explosively flavourful sips, we begin to sag with exhaustion.

On our way home, we stop at the grocery store to pick up some breakfast things, plus a few of John's recommended items — a local sheep cheese and a chicken pot pie — and a couple of bottles of wine, which takes ages because my dad wants something *interesting* and that requires the close reading of labels, the returning and rereading of bottles previously put down, and the comparing of prices. Thanks to the jolly glaze that *Fuck Art the Heathens Are Coming* has poured over my psyche, I find the whole scene gently amusing.

By the time we shuffle and clink everything back to John's flat, we are both ready to drop, but my dad thinks it's still too early to go to bed if we want to adjust to local time, so he suggests we have *a little glass of wine* and watch the news before calling it a night. While I pour two glasses of carefully chosen rosé, he fires off an email to his partner.

My dad and Michael have been together for thirty-five years, mostly happily, always stably and largely conventionally, if we employ typical M norms (Monogamy and Mortgage) as the definition of conventional. It was Michael's decision not to come to Dublin, and he was quite happy to watch my dad and me go off without him. He has done the Genealogy Journey a couple of times already and was keen to let me take over the role of research assistant. *Oh, you'll love it!* he assured me with an exaggerated smile as he waved us off. *As long as you love drizzle and throttling boredom!*

"I'M TELLING MICHAEL THAT IT WAS SO SUNNY TODAY WE BOTH GOT TERRIBLE SUNBURNS," my dad bellows, his fingers bashing the keyboard. I've never understood why he feels the need to raise his voice when he's on the computer, but he always does, as if he were listening to loud music on headphones and had to shout to hear himself.

"WHAT IS THE NAME OF THIS DISTRICT AGAIN?" he calls, as though I were down the hall with the bedroom door closed.

"IT'S CALLED SMITHFIELD," I reply loudly, but he misses the joke.

"I'M TELLING HIM YOU HAVE A BIT OF HEAT STROKE, BUT OTHER THAN THAT EVERYTHING'S FINE," my dad reports, giggling as he types. "WHY DON'T YOU SEE IF YOU CAN FIGURE OUT HOW WE CAN WATCH THE BBC NEWS ON THE TELEVISION SET."

I can't remember the last time I heard someone call it *the television set*, but it suits John's billboard-sized TV and its matching set of controls. I pick up a remote with each hand, begin kneading the squishy plastic buttons while pointing the remotes at different boxes (and eventually at my own head), but I cannot figure out which does what.

"You might have to do without tonight," I tell my dad, a news junkie.

"TRY DOING A BBC INCANTATION WHILE YOU PRESS THE BUTTONS," he suggests, not looking up from his computer.

I close my eyes and chant *BeeeeeeBeeeeeeCeeeeee* in a gravelly baritone while pointing both remotes at the screen.

It doesn't work.

But it does give me an idea to add to my Smart Business Ideas — *Invent Remote Controls That Speak, Telling People Exactly Which Buttons to Press in What Order* — and just as I am bashing the controls on the sofa, trying to turn the damn thing on, the BBC News leaps to life on the screen.

It's spooky.

My dad looks over, nonchalant. "WHAT DID I TELL YOU."

We squeeze onto the narrow sofa and stretch out our legs, splaying our rank and weary feet all over Stephen Harper's tanned hide. It is an extremely satisfying sensation. Within minutes, I feel my dad's head tilt gently onto my shoulder, and by the time the latest should-be-fiction of the U.S. Republican primary race has been discussed by a semicircle of baffled pundits, he is asleep beside me again.

SUNDAY

~⌒

10 BOW STREET

John's toaster doesn't work. The timing mechanism seems to have broken, so unless you keep an eye on the machine and manually expel every slice, it burns the bread to an inedible crisp and produces masses of smoke. My dad is trying to scrape the blackest bits with a sharp knife, but his left arm keeps swirling involuntarily and eventually the toast crumbles to pieces in the sink.

We haven't spent that many mornings together over the last few years. There have been plenty of evenings around his and Michael's dinner table, holiday meals at my brother's, lunches at our place, but this day-to-day living isn't something we've shared for a while. And I've been looking forward to it. In fact, as far as I'm concerned, this whole genealogical mission is just an excuse to spend time together. I'm acutely aware that life as we know it could shift in an instant, so I'd be quite happy to spend the entire week burning toast in our pyjamas and occasionally prancing around the city.

"Here — let me have a go," I say, gathering up the burnt bits, cutting two fresh slices of bread, and starting the whole operation over again.

While the new slices are toasting, I recount the story of a friend's roommate at university, a guy who was given the nickname Toast because that was all he ever seemed to eat. Perhaps from overuse, the house toaster was broken in a similar fashion to John's, and Toast was not the sort of person to do anything so logical as keep an eye on the toasting process or set a timer. On the contrary, he was the sort to do something as illogical as pick at flaming hunks of stuck toast with a fork while the machine was plugged in.

Toast deserves to be electrocuted, my friend once commented casually, *but somehow he never is.*

Being students, it never occurred to them to get a new toaster, even though the small, airless kitchen was continually filling up with smoke and the wall and ceiling near the toaster became streaked with soot. Toast simply developed what he termed *an artistic solution to a utilitarian problem*, flinging the burnt and smoking pieces out the window the moment he extracted them, the charcoaled squares creating an attractive pattern on the grass and, later, the snow. When friends would come over for the first time, they would be told the house number and street name but always with the addendum *the yellow brick one with all the toast.*

My dad's eyes dance as he giggles and imagines. "Maybe they're the people who inspired the Burnt Toast Opera!"

The Burnt Toast Opera? At first I don't believe him.

"It's true! It was written by a Canadian composer, a woman from Vancouver, I think. Michael would know. Anyway, it was a comic operetta and some of it took place in a grocery store. I think there was an aria about a frozen fish . . ."

As my dad rubs his forehead and tries to recall the details, I nip back to my bedroom and hunt down my journal. *His Devotion to Opera, Even One about Burnt Toast.* Then I stand for a minute with my

pen in my mouth, tonguing the circular tip of the cap, determined
to come up with something for the other column, a business idea,
anything, anything . . . *Try to Write for Television?* It is a brilliant idea.
Writers actually make money writing for television. I've heard this.
Actual money. I don't know why I haven't thought of this before.

There is only one problem that I foresee and that is that I haven't
really watched TV since I was a teenager, thirty-plus years ago.
Except: the news when I am visiting my father, tennis when I am
visiting my mother, clips of late-night talk show hosts commenting
on American politics, the World Cup finals in Ecuador in 1990, and
Downton Abbey.

It occurs to me that I may not be qualified to write for television.
That a familiarity with the medium might be helpful, even essential.
I draw a line through the whole idea.

By the time I get back to the kitchen, the toast has burned again.

My dad laughs and says not to worry, he'll eat it anyway, so over
a breakfast of charcoal and jam, we discuss our plans for this, our
last full day as tourists before the serious research begins tomorrow.
My dad is flipping through a guidebook and I reach for one of the
tourist magazines John has left for us.

This year is the centenary of the 1916 Easter Rising, the six-day
armed insurrection in which a small number of Irish Republicans
seized key buildings around Dublin, declaring an end to British
rule and the establishment of an independent Irish republic. The
rebellion was botched, doomed from the beginning for a host of
reasons, and put down in only six days. Of the nearly 3,500 people
taken prisoner by the British, 1,800 of those were sent to intern-
ment camps or prisons, and fourteen of the leaders were executed
for treason and remain celebrated martyrs to this day. *All changed,
changed utterly,* Yeats wrote of the rebellion in his poem "Easter,

1916," memorializing the event with the famously ambiguous line *A terrible beauty is born.*

There are a number of Easter Rising tributes taking place all over the city: films, photo exhibits, tours of some of the key sites. In addition to that, there is Dublin Castle to explore, the Chester Beatty Library, which the *Lonely Planet* calls "not only the best museum in Ireland, but one of the best in Europe," housing impressive collections of rare books, ancient texts, and illuminated manuscripts. And, of course, there is the Guinness Storehouse and Brewery Tour, the most popular tourist attraction in Dublin, and a tour of this very building, the Jameson Distillery.

I list these options aloud.

My dad nods noncommittally, then looks up from his guidebook.

"What about the *Jeanie Johnston?*" he suggests. "It's a replica of a sailing ship that took Irish migrants to North America during the Great Famine. Your ancestors would have taken a boat just like that when they immigrated to Canada."

I am smiling and nodding. I am also plumbing my body for even one drop of excitement about this plan. As hard as it is for me to understand my dad's passion for genealogy and ancestry, it is equally difficult for me to understand my own utter indifference.

I was fortunate enough to know both of my maternal grandparents and I am affectionately curious about my father's parents: who they were, where they came from, what they loved — feminist opinions and debates at the dinner table, apparently, bless their progressive souls — and even who *their* parents were. But once there is a need to count the greats on the fingers — your great-great-great-great-grandfather farmed a small plot in County Sligo, for instance — or once we're beyond first cousins or the term *removed* gets involved (as in, *she would be your great-great-great nephew's wife's fifth cousin twice-removed*), I can feel myself scrabbling away like a cat trying to get out of a bath.

Many people would be intrigued to learn who their Irish great-great-great-great-grandparents were, whether or not they farmed (safe guess: yes), how big the plot was, in what parish, whether the lease is extant, and where that unreadable document is housed. Now more than ever before, I wish I were one of those people.

I should say that I've tried.

I should say it twice: I have *tried*.

For decades, my dad has shared, with ebullient enthusiasm, his successes in locating the gravestones, family crests, photocopies of eighteenth-century birth records, illegible microfilm photographs of death certificates, branches and twigs of family trees, suspected coats of arms, and even a sword used in the Napoleonic Wars by my great-great-great-great-great somebody-or-other. (The weapon is mounted, a bit menacingly I've always found, over a doorway in my dad's house.) He first developed an interest in ancestry when he was still a graduate student, but since retiring he has tackled it with almost obsessive zeal, scouring archives, corresponding with distant relations, joining genealogical societies and websites, and having his DNA analyzed. Twice. While I can summon as much interest as the next person for the source of it all, the universal *Who am I and where do I come from?*, a vague and hypothetical answer is enough for me.

This is not sufficient for my dad.

And that's why we're here, I remind myself. So it's important that I offer all the energy I can to this expedition.

"Okay, the *Jeanie Johnston* it is!" I say with artificial but determined eagerness.

My dad bolts up. "Okay!"

He's still in his nightshirt, a pale-blue, striped, knee-length thing that makes him look the very picture of a nursery rhyme character — *Wee Willie Winkie runs through the town, upstairs downstairs in his nightgown* — and, though I've seen him wear the get-up countless times before, there is something especially adorable about it this morning. He's lost weight, I've noticed, and lately he's been joking about how much shorter he's become, but standing here together in our bare feet I notice it's true: he's not much taller than I am now. He used to tower; suddenly he's petite. It's both impossible and undeniable.

He smiles and squeezes my arm. "Isn't this fun?" he says before scurrying past and knocking me into a memory, a time when I was not much taller than his thigh.

It was the summer we were at family camp in Algonquin Park, a week when parents and kids were invited to use the cabins and facilities of what was normally a camp just for boys. My memory is of the final night revue, for which my dad had written satirical choral music that referenced some of the week's events. He had roped a dozen or so parents into being his choristers and had them all clad in green garbage bags, though the reason for that costuming choice escapes me. What I do remember is that my dad didn't conduct but sang as part of the chorus line, and that he was belting out his absurd song with such gusto and panache — how to describe the extent to which my dad throws himself into things? — he might as well have been on a Broadway stage. In his own mind, I believe he was. The audience was roaring with laughter, wiping their eyes and banging the tables, the whole dining hall reverberating with joy.

I recall looking around at everyone and taking that in, the effect my dad was having on people, the levity they felt, the hilarity he was spinning. I must have been about seven or eight, for it was well before that kind of thing would become embarrassing, before I would wish he were more like other dads, more subdued, more . . . macho. At that time, all I felt was awe, a pride that inflated me to such a degree I felt I might burst — and did, exploding from my seat in the audience, catapulting myself into the middle of the performance, running at my dad, and wrapping my arms tightly around his thighs.

He did not miss a note. He simply placed his hand on my head and continued singing, his whole body bouncing and bobbing with the effort, his voice like a gazelle. Almost immediately, I regretted my move. The song seemed to go on for an eternity. There were so many verses. And I can still summon the saggy chemical stench of that garbage bag, the sweaty scrunch of dark plastic against my cheek. But I also remember how powerful my dad felt, how much energy he had. It was like being attached to a rocket. It was a kind of flying. It was ebullience and rapture, gaiety and sparkle, jubilation, the fullness of life.

It was my dad at his finest.

~

By the time I emerge from the memory, he has changed out of his nightshirt and is ready to go, though halfway down John's narrow hallway he remembers an email he needs to send, so he tells me to go on ahead, we'll meet outside.

And my god, it's sunny *again*. Not warm, exactly, but sunny. Sort of. The sky isn't blue, but it looks as if it might consider that shade for a future occasion.

Well, wait. In the time it's taken me to write that, it's become chilly and grey.

People are in wool coats, women in short skirts and sheer black tights, an outfit that feels more like a protest — *up yers, drizzle* — than clothing that makes any sense in this climate. The men are in sweaters, jackets, nothing particularly notable, and people are the way people are in cities the world over: rushing to get somewhere other than where they are.

In the time it's taken me to write *that*, it's started to spit. And by the time I've flipped to the back of my journal and added *His Wee Willie Winkie Nightgown*, it's hard, lashing rain. I stow everything in my purse and put up my umbrella.

"It was nice a minute ago," I say when my dad joins me on the street.

"That's the nice thing about Irish weather: it might be nice again in another few minutes!" my dad replies. Which might be called the glass half-full approach to meteorology.

As he fumbles with his umbrella, I notice that the tremor in his arm seems to have disappeared. "It's the medication," he explains when he sees me noticing. "Look . . ." He holds out his hand and it is perfectly still.

"That's incredible, wonderful . . ." I say, then hesitate, ". . . isn't it?"

"Well, yes," he answers, lowering his arm and looking disappointed. "But it'll wear off in a couple of hours."

I want to ask more, about the medication, how often he takes it, if there are any side effects and what happens if it loses its efficacy. I have so many questions, but it doesn't feel like the moment. It feels like the moment to wander around Dublin together without a care in the world. So we do that instead.

∽

Within a few blocks we are back at the Liffey, the river that bisects Dublin and pulls softness through this small stone city. Its presence calms the place instantly, as living water does, and it stretches our eyes, sends them skipping from bridge to bridge, cupola to spire. We walk the wooden boardwalks that line the river, leaning into each other and remarking on buildings as we spot them: the imposing neoclassical Four Courts building, current home of the Supreme Court and one of the sites of intense fighting during the Easter Rising of 1916.

"Yes, and then it was nearly completely destroyed a few years later during the Civil War," my dad notes, stepping back to get a full view of the columned facade. "In fact, the Irish Public Record Office used to be housed in a wing of this building and all sorts of documents were destroyed in the fighting. Apparently, the boxes were just being piled in the windows like sandbags. Some of the records dated back to the thirteenth century!"

We continue along the boardwalks until we reach a busy intersection.

"Oh, now this must be O'Connell Street," my dad says, lifting his umbrella and peering down a broad boulevard with expansive sidewalks. "The General Post Office is up on the left. That's where the worst of the Easter Rising took place. The rebels used it as their main base until they were forced to surrender." He points with the tip of his umbrella and squints as rain pours off the edge. "And you'll be interested to know that in the early 1800s, your great-great-great-great-grandfather had a medical practice across the road at number thirteen, though in those days it was called Sackville Street."

"Ah."

"His name was Thomas Egan. His uncle Boetius was the archbishop of Tuam in County Galway. And it was Thomas Egan's daughter who married Henry Faunt." He places emphasis on the surname, adding, "You know who that is."

I hesitate. Feel twelve years old again. "Uhhh . . ."

"It's Henry Faunt's sword that hangs in the dining room," he prompts.

"Over the doorway," I add quickly.

"Yes, another day we should go and see if we can find number thirteen, so you can see where your great-great-great-great-grandfather had a medical practice. Thomas Egan was a graduate of Montpellier University and a member of the Royal Society." He pauses for a moment before adding, "He is our most distinguished ancestor."

The light changes and my dad joins a cluster of pedestrians hustling across the street. But I am bolted to the sidewalk, paralyzed by that great and eternal philosophical question: *Who the fuck cares?* My great-great-great-great-grandfather was a graduate of Montpellier University and a member of the Royal Society. How

on Earth does this matter, in any way, to anyone? And, more immediately, why should it matter to me? Am I meant to feel dignified
by association? Biologically predisposed to studiousness in French?
How to feel anything but wholly indifferent? I do want to try to
develop an understanding of this, to join my father in this pursuit
and be of use to him while we're here, but how exactly am I meant
to connect with this? He was our most distinguished ancestor. What
does that even *mean*? Why would I care?

Well, the quick logic is that my father cares about this stuff,
deeply, and I care about my father, so there we are. What it means
to him and why are mysteries I may never understand, but I can care
because he cares. Simple as that.

I hop off the sidewalk and jog across the wet street, joining my
dad on the other side.

CUSTOM HOUSE QUAY

The *Jeanie Johnston* is what they call a tall ship, though it seems small to my eye — a small-tall ship — particularly when I picture it out in the middle of the Atlantic in a storm.

"Your ancestors would have crossed on a ship much like this one!" my father announces, gesturing at the ship's three masts as we approach the harbor. "The crossings took about six weeks and disease ran rampant." The word *rampant* gallops from his mouth and he flares his eyes. "Imagine being stuck down in the hull of a ship that size for six weeks with people all around you dying of typhoid! And we complain about being on an airplane for six hours beside someone with a cold!"

We push into the ticket office and shake out our umbrellas. Two men look up from the counter. One is weary and pasty. He has eaten corned beef and cabbage for the last one hundred nights in a row and has just learned it will be served again tonight. Something like

that, anyway. The other man is cheerful, sparky. Asks us where we're
from and seems delighted when my dad says Toronto.

"Home to a great many Irishmen," the sparky man says with a
smile.

"Oh, yes," my father replies, nodding with such enthusiasm that
his whole body gets involved. "Some of our ancestors are Irish."

The weary man gets up and leaves the room. He has heard that
sentence three hundred thousand times before.

Sparky nods. "Is dat right?"

"They were from County Sligo and County Galway," my father
adds.

Sparky nods again. Changes the subject. Tells us he's heard about
our new prime minister and that he seems like a right good lad.
"Trudelle? Trudame?"

"Trudeau, yes, Justin Trudeau. His father, Pierre Trudeau, was
prime minister from 1968 to 1979 and then again from 1980 to 1984,"
my father says, his hands cutting the air as he lays out the dates. "His
son Justin won a majority this past October, beating out Stephen
Harper's Conservatives, who were in power for a decade — a *long*
decade," he adds with a grumble of laughter. "It's a relief to have
the Liberals back in power, and so far they seem to be living up to
expectations."

Sparky is blinking. A lot.

I reach over the ticket counter and touch his arm. "My dad's a
retired professor of political science."

Sparky slaps the desk, whistling as he exhales. "Well, that explains
it! I was wondering there as you were going on and on. It was like
watching the telly! Very impressive, sir. Very impressive."

My father smiles and shrugs, looks bemused. He's never seemed
to notice that he speaks in conversational lectures. Or that the rest
of the world doesn't. I used to think he was showing off, being inten-
tionally patronizing. But the day I overheard him responding to my
six-year-old son's innocent query — *what's* govermint? — with a

patient explanation that included the term *Westminster parliamentary system*, I realized that that's just how my dad explains things.

I take a moment at the back of the ticket office to jot that down — *His Professorial Way of Explaining Things* — while my dad asks about the current situation with the Irish government.

Sparky laughs and stands up out of his chair, waving his hands like someone trying to clear smoke. "Janey Mack! I wouldn't dream of having a go at that with the likes of you, sir! I'd come off sounding thick as a plank!"

My father laughs, nervous chuckles that have a woodpecker quality to them, and I can tell he has no idea what has just been said or why. I suggest we go out and join the line for the next tour, which will begin in five minutes. The rain has stopped again, the sky brightening.

"Sunny ways!" my father announces, turning back to the ticket man and explaining, with gusto, the unofficial motto of the new Trudeau government. "Justin used the term in his acceptance speech on election night right after learning he'd won a majority! It was meant as a kind of assurance to Canadians that after a decade of Harper's dirty politics — secrecy, manipulation, contempt for democratic institutions and science, among other legacies — the country would be returning to a more compassionate and reasoned phase of political existence."

Sparky looks as if he's just been whacked in the face with a large book.

"That sounds grand," he says weakly.

My father and I push outside.

We line up along the quay behind two dozen high school students from Milan, all of whom wear stylish shoes and seem blithely aware of how wonderful they look. Their teacher is a gay porn model in his spare time, could be anyway, sculpted and casually attractive, leaning against the railing at the water's edge in a tight leather jacket and scarf, and watching his students with a look of amused insouciance.

Travelling around Ireland with twenty-four teenagers is, apparently, relaxing business.

My dad brings his hand to his mouth and leans into me. Even before he speaks, I know exactly what he is going to say.

"He's very cute," he whispers.

I've been hearing that remark since I was a teenager. My dad would be admiring some model in a clothing ad, some actor in a film, some pretend-person in whatever-it-was, and I'd steel myself, waiting for it. *He's very cute*, he would say with a feather-tickle in his voice, a ripple of pleasure.

I used to hate it. Feel sickened by it. Nauseated, hot-faced, furious. He was out of the closet by then, but I wasn't (open about him to anyone, that is), so I still lived beneath the sticky gauze of shame. When my dad would make the remark, it was playful, as if we were both in on the same joke, sharing the same bit of fun. And being a teenage girl, much of the time I *agreed*. But it was all too much, too weird, and it took time, years, before the comment did anything but infuriate me. I don't remember when I began to find it endearing.

"And here I thought you were having a funereal moment, thinking about our ancestors and how they must have felt prior to boarding one of these ships," I scold him.

My dad straightens up. "Oh, well, of course I was thinking that at first. But then something else caught my eye . . ."

Sparky appears and opens a small gate to the dock. The Italian students shriek and laugh as they walk the gangplank to the ship, clutching each other to stay upright. Their teacher combs his hair back and trails them casually. My dad follows closely behind.

"I'm in deep contemplation about our ancestors!" he whispers over his shoulder.

An American woman on the tour falls in beside me and clutches my arm. "I'm doing the same thing as your father," she tells me soberly, her head down, eyes on her running shoes.

Midway along the gangplank, a young man with a tanned face

turns and looks up at the quayside. "Evvy!" he calls to a girl still standing at the iron railing. She doesn't reply, and the boy is jostled by the flow of his fellow students, who nudge him affectionately, teasing him and knocking his hat off his head until he disappears under a flurry of arms.

~

Our tour begins on the ship's deck with the news that in her day, the original *Jeanie Johnston*, of which this boat is a replica, sailed back and forth across the Atlantic, taking immigrants to North America and transporting timber back to Ireland. A typical voyage took forty-seven days.

Sparky, or Patrick, as he calls himself, has a dramatic way of speaking, drawing out each sentence for maximum effect and letting the tone plummet at the end — *a typical voyage took . . . FOR — ty — se — ven — days.*

"Her maiden voyage was on the twenty-fourth of April, 1848, with one hundred and ninety-three passengers on board. To put that number into perspective," he intones, "it might be helpful to know that with the safety standards of the present day, this ship is licensed to carry . . . only FORTY people . . . including . . . de crew."

Most of us take a moment to look up and down the ship. It is attractive, well crafted, and it reminds me very much of a bath toy I had as a child. The moment our parents were out of sight, my older brother and I would reach for the chunky pink bottle of bubble bath and tip it over carefully, pouring extra dollops of unctuous liquid into the bathtub before churning the water with our small arms, creating masses upon masses of bubbles. Into this maelstrom we would drop our small wooden sailing ship and watch it bob around. Then we'd inflate ourselves, inhaling until our chests felt they would burst, and take turns blowing into the tiny cotton sails. The ship would be sent crashing into the frothing waves, left to struggle to hold itself upright. My brother and I would practically hyperventilate, gasping and blowing until the ship began to tilt, falter, list, pitch, and, eventually, to our shrieks of delight, capsize.

"She would go on to make a total of sixteen crossings between the years 1848 and 1855 . . . bringing more than twenty-five hundred immigrants safely to the New World." Patrick continues, employing pauses to great effect:

"And I am very happy to report . . .

. . . that unlike the vast majority of ships like her . . .

. . . she would not see the death . . .

. . . of a single one . . .

. . . of those passengers."

Patrick lowers his head.

"If you'll follow me now . . . below deck."

Even the Italian students have become serious, less focused on their footwear. Their teacher looks both sexy and pleased, but my dad seems to be entranced by the tour. He walks ahead of me with his head down.

The space below deck is horrifically cramped. A rough wooden bunk that might be called queen-sized would sleep an entire family of six to eight, we are told, with strong preference given to the upper berths. When Patrick asks the students if any of them could guess why, one of the boys says something to his friends in Italian and mimes someone vomiting.

"Right you are," Patrick says, allowing a smile to swim briefly across his face. "You'd not want to be sleeping below with someone ill above you. And between the sea sickness and the dysentery, much could pass from the beds above" — he gestures to the slats of wood forming the top bunk — "to those below."

The stench must have been appalling down here. An acrid, airless, diseased, claustrophobic reek.

"During Ireland's Great Famine, between the years 1845 and 1852, the staple crop of the vast majority of the Irish people was the potato" — *de pedayduh* — "so when it was wiped out by disease, the consequences were devastating. Within seven years, one million out of a total population of eight million people would die of starvation and related causes. Another one million would emigrate on ships such as this one. And the saddest part of all, my friends, is that this starvation was both needless and preventable. For while the Irish people were starving, their precious potato crop rotten with blight, ships full of meat and other food crops . . .

. . . were being continually . . .

. . . exported . . .

. . . to England."

Patrick pours his solemnity onto face after face.

My ignorance roars up. I had no idea food was being exported from Ireland while a million people starved and another million fled the country. Had no idea that the population still hadn't returned to what it was before the famine, not even close. It was eight million in 1850? It's only five million now. Why don't I know any of this?

When I tune back into Patrick's monologue, he is reminding us of the perfect record of the *Jeanie Johnston*, the only famine ship, as they were known, on which not a single passenger's life was ever lost.

Patrick spreads silence around the room, makes eye contact with every member of his audience. "And how, you might wonder, was this ship able to maintain such a record for safety? Indeed, it is a very fine question. And it bids me to explain that the overcrowding of vessels such as these was sadly common in those days, for there was no shortage of people willing to leave the devastation of Ireland and, I'm sorry to say, a great many ship owners who were not as generous of heart as our respectable Nicholas Donovan. As a result, many an immigrant made the journey to the New World without proper sanitation or ventilation, aboard ships that were rife with illness and disease. Thousands perished on those perilous journeys, their bodies thrown overboard . . . to be buried . . . at sea."

He bows his head and nods. A few of the Italian boys do as well.

"The Passengers Act of 1848, a copy of which you'll see there on the wall, outlined the regulations and conditions prescribed to ensure safe passage for immigrants to North America, and Nicholas Donovan made sure to follow this act to the letter. In addition to a very fine captain, Captain James Attridge, the ship would also have a qualified doctor aboard every voyage, and our good Dr. Richard Blennerhassett insisted on the highest standards of cleanliness and sanitation. He would ensure that hatches were opened, accommodations cleaned, and bedding aired and disposed of, when necessary." (I feel better just hearing this.) "And to his great credit, the very fine Dr. Blennerhassett also encouraged a daily walk above deck for every passenger, meaning . . . that in addition to decent living quarters below, every man, woman, and child was given access . . . to salubrious doses . . . of the fresh . . . sea . . . air."

Patrick should be nominated for an Academy Award. His delivery is brilliant, so charged with emotion and immediacy that I feel as if the famine just ended last week.

"Dr. Blennerhassett would continue his service of passengers on the high seas until 1854, when, very sadly, my friends, while on board another emigrant ship, our good doctor would contract cholera and pass away when he was still but a young man . . . of thirty-six . . . years of age." Patrick's eyes are cast down to his hands, which are clasped. He presses his lips together, a gesture of both sadness and satisfaction at what he is able to share with us next.

"But I am very happy to report that our great Captain Attridge would go on to live . . . to the very excellent age . . . of eighty."

My dad, who will soon be the very excellent age of eighty himself, is sitting on one of the wooden benches around a table at the centre of the room. I can see the back of his head and it startles me, as if I am watching time fold, an edge of it suddenly visible. My dad has thick dark curly hair like my own, has always been known for that, recognized in a crowd by it, as often teased as praised for his untameable, wiry black curls. The closely shorn white head by the table isn't my father's at all. Until time unfolds again, and somehow it is. And somehow my dad is suddenly, quietly, eighty. Smaller than he used to be and stooped a bit, at once unrecognizable and intimately familiar.

And invisible, as people of age speak of being, to the young, to the world. The details of their lives and uniqueness lost to the fast glances and reverence of youth. I look around at the Italian students and realize that when they look at my father, they do not see his vivacity, his playfulness, contagious good humour, mad-professor black curls. Of course they don't. What they see is a tremulous old man with shorn white hair sitting quietly on a bench.

The realization feels as monstrous as it does obvious.

∼

We are offered a chance to look around, perhaps read the Passengers Act or walk around and get a feel for the ship. I see my dad enter into discussion with Patrick, no doubt asking a question, so I walk closer to a poster on the wall beside me, something that would have hung in the ship at the time. *Advice to Irish Emigrants*, it's called.

> *In the United States, labour is there the first condition of life, and industry is the lot of all men. Wealth is not idolized; but there is no degradation connected with labour; on the contrary, it is honourable, and held in general estimation.*
>
> *In the remote parts of America, an industrious youth may follow any occupation without being looked down upon or*

sustain loss of character, and he may rationally expect to raise
himself in the world by his labour.

In America, a man's success must altogether rest with
himself — it will depend on his industry, sobriety, diligence
and virtue; and if he do not succeed, in nine cases out of ten,
the cause of failure is to be found in the deficiencies of his own
character.

Patrick continues the tour with descriptions of a typical emigrant experience and the consequent severing of family connections. From memory, he recites letters from Irish parents in search of their children and advertisements placed in American newspapers by those in search of lost relatives, one of them from a father looking for his six sons: "Information wanted of the brothers MacMahon from County Clare, who sailed for New York in 1848. Their father, John MacMahon, will be most thankful to any person who would favour him with any tidings of them. The brothers have dark eyes and dark hair, but for young Eamon, whose eyes are a pale blue."

And for just a moment, I try to imagine watching my own son climb onto this ship, to embark on a journey he might well not survive. I try to imagine being the parent left behind with no way of contacting him, perhaps ever, no information about his whereabouts, his survival. I cannot, possibly, imagine any of this, but it feels important — imperative — to try.

We end the tour back on deck, where Patrick takes measured satisfaction in recounting the story of the original ship's ultimate demise in 1858, which sounds like a Hollywood creation but which is, apparently, true. "En route from Quebec with a cargo of timber, she ran into trouble in the middle of the Atlantic and became waterlogged. By necessity, her crew climbed into the rigging, while the ship . . . began to sink . . . into the dark and cold waters . . . of the mid-Atlantic."

It is his final soliloquy. He is giving it everything he's got.

"After *nine* days of clinging to the masts and watching their beloved ship sink slowly beneath them, a Dutch ship by the name of *Sophie Elizabeth* was able to save . . . every . . . last . . . member . . . of the crew. " He squints into the horizon, his voice strung with emotion. "Meaning . . . that even in her final hours, she would maintain her perfect record of safety . . . and her legend . . . would remain . . . pure . . . and true."

If we weren't already standing, we would be rising to our feet. The applause, even from the Italian students, is hearty and prolonged. My dad shouts *Bravo!* and congratulates Patrick several times, telling him what a talented storyteller he is, how captivating. "You had us all right here!" my dad exclaims, cupping his hand in front of him.

Patrick looks delighted, if sheepish, shyly accepting the compliments, but far more awkward in his own skin than he was, only moments ago, as the narrator of the story. Definitely an actor.

～

"Wasn't he terrific!" my dad says as we make our way back up to the street. He is bouncy, his body rebounding like a sprung coil with each step. We are heading back towards the centre of town in search of something to eat, when we come upon a cluster of bronzed ghosts standing in the middle of the sidewalk.

They are life-sized. Gaunt. Some clutch infants and bundles to their chest. Others are hunched, defeated. Withering. All are skeletal. There is a man doubled over with a child draped over his wire-thin back. A woman whose mouth is gaping, her hands on her chest, her eyes on the sky. Haunted. Pleading.

There is a plaque on the ground: *In memory of the victims of the Great Famine and for their descendants who have done so much to build Canada. The Right Honorable Jean Chrétien, Prime Minister of Canada, 1999.*

My dad and I look back at the sculptures.

"It's very effective," he says with a slight quaver in his voice.

It's new, this quaver. He used to be more impervious to things, emotions, plights. But a casing has dropped away in recent years. His voice offers up a vulnerability that wasn't there before.

"And today these people are Syrians."

MONDAY

NATIONAL ARCHIVES OF IRELAND

My father and I are asked to present two pieces of picture iden-
tification and to lock our bags, coats, books, binders, food,
and pens in an adjoining glass room. No pens, the security guard
reminds us, as he hands us two blunt pencils and directs us towards
the lockers. It feels as if we are visiting someone in prison.

The elevator is dark. I expect to walk out into cavernous rooms
filled with balding monks in heavy robes and fragile books from
the fifteenth century, but it's a small, unremarkable room, typical
of any modern library forced to surrender beauty to practicality.
Half the room is devoted to microfilm machines — my eyes yawn
just looking at them — and the shelves are filled mostly with dull
green leather-bound reference books. I have always wondered who
decided that dyeing leather green was a good idea.

Once we've registered and been issued identity cards on chain
lanyards, the registrar suggests that we begin our visit at the office
of the resident genealogical records expert.

Mary Derry is the personification of the words *resident genealogical records expert*. Her hair is short, white, and without nonsense. She wears smart, sensible clothing. It is so sensible I forget what it looks like the moment I look away, but it is either beige or grey or navy blue. Her only adornment is a cameo pendant necklace on a thin gold chain. Her bifocals sit in pince-nez position.

My father says good morning in a respectful tone.

"Sign the guest book individually, please," she says without looking up from her desk. Her right hand points to a table on one side of the room.

We grind our names into the book with our blunt pencils and sit in the pair of chairs in front of her desk like schoolchildren in the principal's office.

Mary Derry finishes what she is doing, cross-checking something in a reference volume, before looking up, already fed up with us, and asking how she can be of service.

Before my father has finished his first sentence, she is wincing. But he goes on, explaining that we are looking for information on families by the name of Faunt, Egan, Thompson, and Lougheed from County Sligo, County Westmeath, and County Galway, who immigrated to Canada in the 1830s. He outlines the routes he has already taken in search of said information, various online services, visits to libraries in Belfast and Dublin and parish churches all over Ireland a decade ago, plus a visit to the National Archives at Kew a couple of years ago. On this trip, he hopes to find some documents — a marriage settlement, a will, information on possible land holdings — that might help him gain a better understanding of the circumstances of the families. Mary Derry listens with an air of disapproval I imagine she never quite shakes.

She stops short of extending her fingers and slapping him on the nose for expecting to find the documents for which he is searching, but her tone is patronizing enough that the nose slap is implicit.

"One must take into account the paucity of material extant for that period," she says, as though the phrase *paucity of material extant for that period* were normal conversation. Then she reminds him, sternly, of the parish records that were destroyed during the Four Courts fire of 1922 and pronounces that, in any event, the registry of the kind of information he is seeking was entirely optional at the time and, therefore, mightn't ever have existed in the first place.

Oh, yes, he's very aware of all of that, my father assures her, sitting forward in his seat and nodding deferentially, but he wonders if she might be able to suggest some other avenues or be able to help him locate a couple of estate records he has noted. She has a quick look at the titles, winces again, and begins rhyming off suggestions as to where he might start.

At me, she does not gaze at all. Occasionally, I try to catch her eye, but the blunt pencil I used to sign in seems to have released a potion that has rendered me invisible. Part of me is tempted to start moving things around on her desk to see if that gets a response. Before I do, though, I notice that my dad's handwriting is unable to keep up with the suggestions she continues to toss out, like coins to the poor, and I raise an invisible hand and address her for the first time.

"Sorry," I say, leaning forward and pointing to my father's flustered writing, "that was Sir Thomas who?"

She pauses, looks at me over the top of her glasses as if I'd just belched, and then carries on without acknowledging the question. I laugh, because I've always found laughter to be the most effective response to displays to self-importance, and she looks at me again, long enough to take in a quick sip of breath and tighten the belt around the conversation by another notch.

When my father enquires about a particular set of birth records, Mary Derry seems equal parts delighted and peeved to inform him that those records, as identified, are housed in the National *Library*, which is a different institution entirely. She feels the need to repeat that several times. A Different Institution *Entirely*.

At the end of our brief meeting, she sends us, through waves of disapproval, to a counter on the other side of the room, where my father asks the man in charge about birth and death registries for the parishes of Emlaghfad, Aghanagh, Kilcolman, Kilfree, Kilmorgan, and Skreen. The man does not bat an eyelash. On the contrary, he nods, sees my dad's Kilcolman and Kilfree, and raises him a Kilmacallan, Kilmactranny, and a Kilmoremay. All I can think is how good a Kilkenny is going to taste at the end of this day, but in the meantime, while the two of them play out all possibilities for the prefix in question, I busy myself by browsing the bookshelves, flipping, for no particular reason, through the *Surnames Index* and the *Memorials of the Dead*. It is an experience very much like reading the telephone book and I have no idea why I am doing it, other than to look busy while my father lays the groundwork. And to feel useful, though even as I am attempting to look studious, I am well aware that there is nothing useful, at all, about what I am doing.

My dad stays busy with the death registries, so I pull out a short article he wrote recently for a genealogical society newsletter, in which he outlines his plans and hopes for this trip.

> *I have decided to have another go at researching my mother's Irish ancestors. I have already done some research in Dublin and Belfast, but one lives with the hope there will be more nuggets of information just waiting to be discovered. I am being joined by my daughter, Alison, who has not the same degree of interest in family history, but she loves to travel and has never been to Ireland. Maybe she will catch the genealogy bug!*

It's a bit heartbreaking, that last sentence, particularly the exclamation point, because while it's still early days, early hours — it's been less than an hour, actually — I am fairly sure I am psychologically vaccinated against this bug. Though you never know! Maybe

I will catch it! Which would be great! I sit up and open myself to the possibility that I might be surprised, spontaneously infected and feverish, wracked with fervour and genealogical phlegm. Emlaghfad, Aghanagh. Already I can feel it developing.

> We will be researching four families who all immigrated to Canada in the early 1830s. I want to focus my research on answering the questions: Why did they decide to emigrate at that time? What were their circumstances in Ireland that led them to hope for a better life in the backwoods of Upper Canada? The pressures would have been very different from those experienced by Irish emigrants just ten years later, during the Great Famine, when the choice was very stark but simpler: leave Ireland or starve to death.

This is quite interesting, actually, to try to understand what kind of lives these people might have had and to imagine their dreams for a better life in a faraway land. Perhaps there is hope of catching this bug after all.

> I don't know much about Robert Lougheed and his family in County Sligo. They apparently lived in Tiraree in the parish of Kilmorgan, but this has not been confirmed. He seems to have had a connection with Ballymote because, when he was asked to name the post office in London [Ontario] Township, he called it Ballymote. A Dr. Joseph Lougheed lived in Ballymote and died in 1869, aged seventy-six years. He may have been a relation of Robert. There is some evidence suggesting that Robert had four siblings in Canada: Margaret, David, William, and Warren (whose mother Jane lived with him). Robert's wife, Jane Henry, was the youngest daughter of David Henry and Elizabeth Ann Roney of Faughts, parish of Calry in County Sligo.

On second thought, I'm fairly sure I'm immune, because there are only so many paragraphs like that I am willing to read in my lifetime. All those lifeless names, those story-less places and dates. Despite my best efforts, I can feel myself tuning out by sentence number three. Which brings us to the Great Divide, the point at which the path to family history always bifurcates and my father and I have always gone scampering off in opposing directions: he in search of dry facts, legal documents, and provable direct descendants, and I in blind pursuit of great stories and characters, whoever the bloody hell they are. But I need to stay focused on his way of doing things, his process of panning for ancestry. I may be more interested in colourful fictions than black-and-white data, but I am determined to find a way into all of this and help discover something significant, facilitate a big discovery, to make this trip fruitful for him.

The other great divide, and there's no solving this one, is that my dad is an academic, with lots of impressive letters after his name. And I'm Not, with None. I did go to university but not, um, very well. What does that mean exactly? Well, in situations such as this one, where research and investigation and theory and critical thought are key players, I believe it means that if there is ever any doubt, I'm probably wrong.

But I could be wrong about that.

It's a bit of a sore point (for me), though far less so now than when I was in my twenties and trying to prove myself, win my dad's approval. I never worked at winning my mother's — I had it always, without question — but I laboured and fought for my dad's, often in peculiar, even counterproductive, ways. He was always loving and accepting, attentive and supportive, so why I so often felt I was landing shy of expectation I was never quite sure.

It's possible I still do. And I'm still not quite sure why.

I watch my dad tie up a conversation with one of the archivists and gather his papers. He waves me towards the door. Wouldn't you know it, Mary Derry was right: there's nothing here for us. The records we are searching for do not seem to exist in this building, the National Archives, but rather at the National Library.

"So, what is it *exactly* that we're looking for?" I ask as we wait for the elevator.

My dad produces such a dramatic full-body sigh that he practically doubles over.

I lean forward, touch his arm, feel incompetent already. "Sorry! It's that you've never really said."

"No-no, no-no," he says, straightening up. "It's just that there's no simple answer. Or, rather, the simple answer is that I don't really know."

I'm not sure how to greet this news. I decide to nod.

My dad takes a deep breath. "By that I mean that we often don't really know what will be useful until we stumble on it. And my experience with this type of research is that I might think I'm looking for one thing, but in the search for it something unexpected can be unearthed. In the simplest terms, though, it's what I told the woman earlier: we're looking for information about my mother's ancestors, specifically the four families who all emigrated from different parts of Ireland in the 1830s, a decade before the Famine."

"And you'd like to know why they decided to emigrate then."

He nods, ready to end the conversation there.

"But what will that *look* like? What exactly is *information about your mother's ancestors?*"

He sighs again, deeply and expansively. "Well, I suppose the ideal might be a letter, say, from a relative who had already settled in Canada and might have been encouraging more family members to join them. Or a lease that showed how much land a family had in Ireland, or perhaps a deed. Or a marriage settlement — now that would be terrific. Those tend to have a lot of information on them: names of parents, the parish, the county. Or a will . . ."

He can see me wilting at the sound of the words *leases, deeds, marriage settlements, wills.*

"Think of it as a kind of archaeological dig!" he suggests, making wide arcs with his arms in an attempt to liven things up, keep me enthused. "There will be a lot of sifting through sand looking for bones and pottery shards . . . And while you might not be able to detect which discoveries are pertinent, you can help with the digging!"

I smile. He is trying to engage the adventurer in me. I am trying equally hard to locate my inner scholar.

"Now, I did some of this research when Michael and I were in Ireland ten years ago, but I was quite rushed and I'm sure there was a lot I overlooked. We'll need to be very efficient," he says, becoming suddenly stern. "There is a *lot* of ground to cover. And we don't have much time."

"Six days."

"Five *and a half* days," he corrects me. "Everything closes at noon on Saturday."

He checks his watch. Presses the elevator button again.

The bell dings and the elevator doors open, but just as he is stepping in, my dad turns to me with a look of concern. "What about your Burmese prince?"

I find it so touching that he's remembered.

"You go and have a look. I'll wait over here," he says, stepping out and pointing to a bench by the wall.

"I'll be quick," I say, jogging back to the main reference desk, where a man with the voice and demeanour of a bullfrog asks what he can do for me.

I explain that I am looking for a letter from a Burmese prince and show him the information. The man raises his eyebrows grandly, revealing an even greater resemblance to a bullfrog in the process, and waves over a colleague who is tall and thin and buttoned to the neck. This man runs his finger along the information and pronounces something confidently, definitively, but his accent coils and twists so tightly around the words that I am unable to extract a single one. After a bit more croaking and coiling on the man's part and some leaning and straining on my own, a third man approaches and explains, most regretfully, that the numerical cataloguing which I possess does, in fact, indicate that the document for which I am searching will require a visit to the National *Library*.

"Which is a different institution entirely," I say like an expert.

The three men smile and speak in unison:

"'Tis."

NATIONAL LIBRARY OF IRELAND

I am encircled by pudgy, dimpled knees and stubby penises. *Cherubs,* I said a moment ago, only to be corrected by a young man beside the circulation desk, who called it an honest mistake.

They're actually putti, he whispered, pointing to the softly lit sculptures above the bookshelves. *True cherubim,* he continued, *have four animal faces and numerous sets of wings. A winged boy is a putto. A beautiful, ineffectual dreamer.* He paused, tilted his head, winced. A look of pity. *Honest mistake,* he reassured me. *Most of the world makes it.*

I thanked him for the clarification. Turned to my dad, who flared his eyebrows playfully and gestured to the centre of this majestic round room. We took slow, creaking steps to the nearest empty long desk and settled into furniture so elegant it felt like a privilege.

It must be fifty feet to the top of the great dome under which we sit, dozens of us, in rows and rows of handsome antique desks. Small dark-green glass lamps curve elegantly over each workspace, but not a single one is on. The natural light singing down from a ring of arched windows around the dome is enough, is more than enough. It is vaulted light within a poetry of rounded space, as uplifting as it is illuminating.

The room is study-quiet. It holds the sound of people plunging into the pages of books and swimming back through centuries. There is such quiet harmony in this rotunda I am enlivened just sitting in it.

The only trouble is that I always seem to arrive at places like this with intestinal gas. I can never figure out what everyone else does with theirs. With all exits squeezed tightly, I can hear the vapours recycling themselves through all the available pipes and channels. Everyone around me hears the same. So I'm self-conscious, but I like it here. Like the creaky wood floors and the pleasure of crafted furniture, the care and attention that has gone into detail: the bas-reliefs over the doorways, the chubby bellies of the *putti*, the intricate carvings on the legs of the desks, the chairs, the visual arpeggio of the dome, the way a part of me takes flight when I look up into it.

Apart from *helping with digging*, it's still not clear what my actual tasks will be as research assistant, but until I get my bearings, learn the geography and terminology, stop accidentally referencing women's reproductive organs, et cetera, I am simply taking cues from my father and helping in whatever way I can. A moment ago, I filled out all the requests for material, for instance, as my dad's handwriting has been illegible for as long as I've been alive and seems to be getting worse. I used to think it looked like a cross between the results of an EKG machine and the Lascaux cave paintings. My brother used to call it hand barf. Either way, it's difficult to read, so I do the writing and wait for the books to be brought up from wherever they normally live.

We are each permitted to examine only one book at a time, so my father hands me *A Census of Ireland, c. 1789, with Supplementary Material from the Poll Money Ordinances (1788–1791)* and asks me to leaf through it for a reference to the Faunt family — my gr-gr-gr-gr-grandfather, owner of the doorway sword — while he consults a large volume on land tenure. I am glad to have been given a concrete task, though my eyes begin to wander shortly after plodding through the book's title and I am reminded, again, why I dropped out of university as soon as I could.

I locate enough self-discipline to peruse the entire book, return it to the desk, and begin on a second volume, *The Parishes of Aghanagh and Ballynakill: A Complete History*, which is exactly as readable as it sounds. My third volume is the runaway bestseller *South Half-Barony of Tirerrill: Summer Assizes, 1835: Presentments*, but the fourth book, *In Sligo Long Ago*, is encouraging, suggesting as it does the presence of an actual narrative.

> *The rot in the potato resembles cholera — and like it, it will not be arrested until it has destroyed a certain portion of the crop. "Indian corn" or maize was brought from America. It became known as "Peel's brimstone," partly because of its bright sulphur yellow colour, and partly because of its effects on the digestive system.*

I make a mental note to avoid dishes containing maize while I am at work in the Reading Room of the National Library of Ireland and then my eyes snag on the first non-soporific paragraph of the day.

> *William Taylor, an inmate of Sligo Workhouse, submitted the following application to the Board of Guardians, February, 1858:*

Ye muses from Parnassus hill,
I pray ye now assist my quill,
To spin a simple rustic verse,
And let the gents know my distress,
And hopes the Board will not refuse,
To grant to me a pair of shoes,
The farmers then will me employ —
The skin won't do on spade on cloy.
The Lord of Heaven will ye bless
To help a brother in distress
Kind gentlemen of highest fame,
My poor request do not disclaim,
I hope it will not meet a failure
Your humble servant —
William Taylor.

I am enchanted. Did all the men in the Sligo workhouse write like this? Who was this William Taylor and what became of him? It's all so surprising, his appeal to the muses of Parnassus hill, sacred mountain of Greek mythology — how would he have known that? — but it's also pitiful, his need to petition for a pair of shoes in order to escape the workhouse and be hired as a farmhand, not to mention Taylor's choice to rhyme his name with failure. I'm so disheartened by this last detail, in fact, that in honour of William Taylor, poet laureate of·the Sligo workhouse, I stop and run through the alphabet in search of an alternative rhyme.

Bailer . . . nailer . . . paler . . . quail or . . . sailor.

I rewrite the line a few times and test out some of the options.

Kind gentlemen of highest fame,
My poor request do not disclaim,

Would that I would not grow paler
Your humble servant — William Taylor

My boat is sinking I need a bailer
Your humble servant — William Taylor

If only I could shoot a quail or
A duck, yours truly — William Taylor

I am enjoying myself, chuckling at this last version, when my dad asks how I'm coming along.

My imagination tumbles all the way down Parnassus hill as I look over at him.

I have forgotten entirely what I am meant to be doing.

"Have you found any mention of the Lougheeds?" he asks, to which I sputter and admit that I've been caught up by a poem. I slide the book over to his side of the polished wood desk and let him read it, while I look up and let my eyes enjoy a few turns around the dome. My dad finishes the poem, shrugs, and says *huh*, before reminding me that William Taylor is not a relative.

I smooth the page and prepare to return to the family-finding, when I notice a small starred note at the bottom: *Taylor's application was successful.*

He got his shoes! I lean over and whisper the news to my dad, who sighs and says, "Lougheed, Lougheed."

I continue paging through *In Sligo Long Ago* with one eye on the lookout for Lougheeds and the other on furtive watch for William Taylor and more information about the workhouses. Of course, this puts me in the mindset of Dickens, of Oliver Twist, and then I cannot help thinking of the time our high school put on *Oliver!* and I was cast as one of the workhouse boys and the shadow vocalist for the Artful Dodger, who looked the part but couldn't sing. And then, of course, I begin to imagine the story of William Taylor as a musical.

Please, sir, I want some . . . shoes?

There are lots of fun possibilities for choreography, a light-footed bit as he exits the workhouse with his new pair — maybe tap shoes?

My dad clears his throat, as if he could sense the song and dance inside my head, and returns to his reading. Contrite, I strike a studious pose with my elbow on the desk and my forehead in my hand. The phrase *fake it till you make it* swims to mind.

Unfortunately, William Taylor seems to have put on his newly granted shoes and run right off the pages of the book, as there is no further mention of him. But I do learn that the population of Ireland grew from three million in 1780 to a whopping eight million by 1840, thanks largely to the easily grown, vitamin-rich potato, according to the book, which fails to thank the easily enjoyed, hormone-rich act of sex, though I suppose that's implied.

I find it impossible to understand how the potato — the potato! — could be responsible for such an explosion in population, and try as I might to bridle my eyes and trot them around in search of Lougheeds, I feel them pulling my mental bit in search of answers to this mystery.

No great surprise, but as it turns out, this story of starvation is actually a story of greed played out by people with no connection to the land whatsoever. The main players were the landlords, most of whom lived in England and might have visited their land only once or twice in a lifetime, and the middlemen, who were described in an 1845 British Royal Commission report on land laws in Ireland as *the most oppressive species of tyrant that ever lent assistance to the destruction of a country.* The middlemen would lease the land from the absentee landlords and subdivide the bejesus out of it before renting as many teensy tracts as possible to tenants, who became indentured slaves the moment they stepped into the agreement but who, in a feudal society, had few, if any, other options. Conditions were typically appalling, with families often living without beds, blankets, or adequate protection from the elements.

As the Royal Commission reported, *It would be impossible to adequately describe the privations which the Irish labourer and his family habitually and silently endure . . .* adding that they *could not forbear expressing our strong sense of the patient endurance which the labouring classes have exhibited under sufferings greater, we believe, than the people of any other country in Europe have to sustain.*

In addition to working to pay rent to the middlemen, the tenants also had to raise crops and livestock for the landlord, who would export both bounty and profits to England. Only then could the tenants turn around and try to grow enough food to live on. Because the land had been subdivided so many times and the tracts of land were so small, however, the only crop that could be grown in sufficient quantity to feed a family was the potato, particularly the hardy and onomatopoeic variety, the Irish Lumper. It might not have been a complex diet, but it kept people alive and procreating. Until the population was fully and dangerously dependent on the plant and the entire nation's crop became infected with blight.

Nothing spells ecological disaster quite like monoculture and genetic homogeneity, so the stage was set for the blight to run wild when it arrived in Ireland in 1845. That year, almost half of the cultivated acreage in Ireland was diseased. A deputation from the citizens of Dublin was sent to the Lord Lieutenant of Ireland proposing the importation of foreign corn (the infamous Peel's brimstone) and the prohibition of the export of food, but they were told not to be alarmed, that such suggestions were premature, as there was no immediate or significant threat.

By the following year, a full three-quarters of the harvest was rotten, inedible, and tens of thousands were dying of starvation, while food continued to be exported to England for the profit of the landlords. Within two years, a million people had died of starvation and another million had boarded ships like the *Jeanie Johnston* and fled the country in search of a future.

It is hard not to become a revolutionary on the spot. If there were a sign-up sheet at the front desk alongside the requests for material, my name would be on it. But I do not see one. Instead, as I stand, mentally storming the Bastille and waiting for my next book to be retrieved, I notice a small sign entitled *Reader Handling Rules*. They are all fairly standard: *Do not eat or drink while handling the materials. Do not write on any part of the materials*, et cetera, but I particularly like the wording of Reader Handling Rule #10.

Do not moisten a digit to aid in page turning.

Back at our shared desk a few minutes later, my dad's concentration and focus on his book is so impressive, I scratch the words *His Dedication and Focus, Even to the Fantastically Mundane* into my notebook. Then my head begins to bloat with questions. How does he manage to stay interested in lines and lines of names and townships and parishes? How can he keep himself from contracting narcolepsy and falling face first onto the desk? How is it that he has chosen to sit here perusing unreadable books, willingly, when he has the opportunity and resources at this time in his life to go anywhere and do almost anything? Why has he chosen to sit in the National Library of Ireland paging through parish records instead of, say, going on an elephant safari in Sri Lanka? I am confounded, trying, straining to understand, and desperate to establish how it is that I am going to summon and sustain a similar dedication for the next five and a half days, when I notice him lick the tip of his finger and reach for the corner of the page.

"Dad!" I whisper-shout. "Do not moisten your digit to aid in page turning!"

My father wipes his hand on his sleeve before proceeding.

I look around the room proudly. No one else has noticed anything, but it is the first time I feel that my services as research assistant have been of any discernible value.

Which calls for a break.

My dear friend,
Does your research with your dad involve a trip to the National
Archives in Dublin? If so, I am after a letter there written by
a Burmese prince. If you could look it up for me, please let me
know and I will send details.

Longer communication long overdue. I hope all's well with
you. We are all fine here in many respects, though aspects of
21st century life I could do without. I miss those long handwrit-
ten letters — though who's got time to write them nowadays?
Tasha xxx

I met Tasha in 1990 while living in Prague. It was one year after Czechoslovakia's Velvet Revolution and we were both there as teachers, ostensibly, and as imposters, essentially, for like most of the Anglos hired to teach English to the newly de-communized Czechs and Slovaks, neither of us had ever done anything of the sort before. Somehow I landed a job in federal parliament teaching English to members of Václav Havel's first government, and to this day, it's the wackiest job I've ever had. Three times a week, large, pale men would gather around a table at the parliamentary restaurant, order beer and blood sausage at seven in the morning — yes — and wait for me to kick off a conversation in English. For the ensuing hour, I would sip coffee, introduce useful political vocabulary, pass the mustard, correct grammar, and teach handy diplomatic phrases such as, "In my opinion, sir, George Bush is a blowhole."

Tasha never actually moved into my flat on Jaselská Street — she had a teaching post in a town in southern Moravia — but she must

have spent a good deal of time there, for whenever I think back to
that time and that small, high-ceilinged flat, she is there: making
pot after pot of strong black tea, stirring fragrant curry powder into
pans of otherwise tasteless food, pouring pilsner from the metal
bucket we'd fill at the corner pub, theorizing loudly, laughing loudly,
and planning trips to the Soviet Union (as it was then) with a cynical
American, who later fell off a roof and died. I believe she slept in the
kitchen. Yes, she did. For I can picture her pulling herself up from
the bench behind the table like a mythical creature emerging from
the sea, reaching for her thick-lensed glasses, saying *carpe diem*, and
getting up to make tea.

I don't remember meeting Tasha so much as instantly adoring
her, wandering around a faintly dilapidated Prague together, aimless
and curious, so very young. We took spontaneous trips to Bohemian
villages, hiked to mountain pubs, feasted on beer and black bread
and cheese so stinky it had to be kept in a sealed jar outside. Once
we stumbled upon a graveyard of communist statues, a make-
shift repository for the deposed stone renderings of Lenin and his
disciples. It was fun at first, kicking and picking through smashed
bearded heads and toppled communist fists clenched around dogma
and farm implements, until suddenly, for no reason, the scene felt
so eerie that we shrieked and exploded from the place like children
escaping the outstretched fingers of ghosts.

When I decided to leave Prague and take the Trans-Siberian
express to China, it was Tasha I sat down with over Czech plonk and
Indonesian cigarettes to pore over maps and ideas. We read aloud to
each other from travel classics, passages that conjured the ancient
Silk Road, the Taklamakan desert, the crossroads of Kyrgyzstan,
Tajikistan, and Kashmir. And after weeks on trains and collapsing
buses through Russia, Siberia, Mongolia, and across the endless
deserts of northwestern China, I reached the legendary market in
Kashgar, where I sat down on a coarse wooden cart beside a camel
stall and penned a letter to Tasha which began with the word *Arrived*.

Years later, we met up in Spain and trundled through Andalucía together, sopping up olive oil with stale bread and Moorish architecture with starved eyes. Years after that, I put my toddler on my hip and flew to Vietnam, where Tasha was living at the time. A few years after that, she married an Englishman, had two children of her own, and got a job at Cambridge University. Where she is now doing research, evidently, involving a Burmese prince with a connection to Ireland.

I show the information to a ginger, ruddy-cheeked woman at the main desk.

"Happily, you find yourself in the right building but, sadly, at the wrong end of it," she tells me, pouring as many smiles into each word as she can. This is the Reading Room of the National Library, I learn. The *Manuscripts* Reading Room, home to letters by fabled Burmese princes and the like, is out the main building and down the block.

I thank her and make a trip to the toilets, travelling the marble staircase past an earth-toned stained glass window and a sign for the Reading Room translated into Irish, *Seomra na Léitheoieachta*, which wins today's award for Vowel Inclusivity. The women's toilet area includes a large and elegant powder room, I suppose it is, bedecked in mirrors and a velvet divan. Briefly, I recline and eat a piece of chocolate, partly because I happen to have that very thing in my pocket and also because it seems like the appropriate thing to do given the surroundings. As I am stretched out, enjoying the thickening spread of cocoa butter across my tongue and smiling at women who arrive with full bladders and leave with empty ones, I make a mental note to add *Divans/Chocolate Dispensers in Women's Washrooms* to my *Smart Business Ideas* column.

When I climb back upstairs and return to the Seomra na Léitheoieachta, it's two o'clock. My friend from the Cherubim Correction Society is no longer at the reference desk, but I notice a group of young men in the midst of an intense, though whispered, argument. Something about *Hamlet* and whether or not Shakespeare himself was speaking through the character of Hamlet's ghostly father, which would make Anne Hathaway the guilty queen. It's pretentious and nauseating, but I listen anyway.

Until one of the men turns away, distracted by a sound in the centre of the room.

My dad.

Bent over a stack of sepia pages and so engaged in the material, he is unaware that his left arm is flailing wildly and making a loud rhythmic banging on the papers. Eventually, he tucks the shuddering arm behind his back. Where it is still for a moment, a few moments, before starting to tremor again, mildly at first and then fiercely, as if it were a live wire, coiling and lashing. I can feel my eyes filling, my chest shattering.

Part of me wants to march over and make it all stop: aging, decline, that damn tremor, where all of this is going. I want it to stop. I have to make it stop. I clench myself together and stride towards him, every loud creak in the floor feeling like a glass I am smashing to the floor. My dad notices me coming and looks up. Smiles. Suggests we break for lunch.

I nod, exhale, compose myself. "I was just going to propose something like that."

∽

There is a pleasant cafeteria on the library's ground floor. We both order leek and potato soup with Irish soda bread. And all I can say is that there is nothing quite like eating potatoes in a country where a million people died for the lack of them. There is also nothing quite like watching my father's arm quake as it is doing so forcefully at the moment. Twice the bread nearly flies from his hand as he tries to spread it with cold butter.

I'm still unsure how to navigate all of this with him, when to offer help and when to back off and ignore it, as he seems to try to do. I don't want to embarrass him or elbow in on his independence, and I'm not sure if he prefers to do things himself, even when they are difficult.

"Would you like some help?" I ask, only when the butter will not, will *not*, submit to being smoothed onto the bread.

He doesn't look up. "Sure."

· And it's no big deal. I scrape some butter onto a knife and drag it over the grainy nubbles of his bread. We keep talking about what-ever we were talking about — Yeats's mysticism; my dad thinks it's hokey and I find it fascinating — but the whole scene feels amplified: the chunky texture of the butter as it resists puttying the crevices, the smell of the grains in the bread, the roaring intimacy of that moment, and the silent tilting of our world in that casual reach across the table.

∾

In 1817, Dr. James Parkinson wrote "An Essay on the Shaking Palsy," in which he described an *involuntary tremulous motion, with lessened muscular power, in parts not in action and even when supported; with a propensity to bend the trunk forwards, and to pass from a walking to a running pace: the senses and intellect being uninjured.* Two hundred years later, there are between seven to ten million people living with Parkinson's disease worldwide. A chronic and degenerative disease, its symptoms generally worsen over time. Just as the cause is unknown, the cure remains elusive.

∾

When we have scraped the last smear of potato from our bowls, we return to the Reading Room, where a stack of new materials is wait-ing for us. My dad heads off with an *Index of Landlords*, the infamous bastards who brooked the famine and upon whose graves I would like to take my next piss, while I tackle *Diocesan and Prerogative Marriage License Indexes 1623–1866* and its winning cousin *Diocesan and Prerogative Probate Indexes 1595–1858.* I am unsuccessful in finding mention of any of the four families we are searching for in either volume, but I am successful in testing the theory that it is possible to conduct genealogical research while wondering what sort of dessert to have with tea.

My next conquest is *The O'Connors of Ballyṣumaghan: A History* and I am to read it with an eye on conditions and events in the early to mid-1830s, specifically what might have prompted a family to decide to emigrate at that particular time. It's not difficult to understand why people left Ireland during and after the Famine, my dad emphasizes, but why before?

He has a few theories: economic conditions, i.e., the slump following the end of the Napoleonic Wars; religious conflict (at least one of the families we're looking into was Catholic); the opportunity to exchange the life of a subsistence tenant-farmer on a small plot of land for the chance to acquire outright ownership of a large farm in Canada at a moderate price. But it's all conjecture.

The task itself has potential, though the writing in *The O'Connors of Ballysumaghan: A History* is so hopelessly turgid, so stacked with facts, dates, one-dimensional people, and plodding, interminable detail that every page thuds on my mind like a dead tree. It must be because of prose like this that a prison term became known as a sentence.

By the time I'm finished, I've pretty much decided on the lemon square. I report my findings (none) to my dad, who still has quite a ways to go with his current volume, he tells me, his face full of scholarly knots. "There are still the parish registers for baptismal and marriage records to be looked through," he says, pointing to a dark alcove at the back of the Reading Room. "Those are all stored on microfilm."

"Ahhh," I say, jettisoning all fantasies I might have had for the remainder of the afternoon. "The parish records. Right, I'll do those now."

~o

When we planned this trip a few months ago, I did understand that the focus of our time would be genealogy, but only now — just this minute — am I coming to terms with the uncontested prominence of that focus. Naively, perhaps, I'd been assuming there might be a limit to the number of hours my dad would want to spend swotting in libraries, and, what with his age, I suppose I thought that number might be quite small.

My vision had been something more along the lines of an Irish Genealogy Lite package: a few hours every morning in libraries and archives, a long pub lunch, and the rest of the day free to explore the city or wander the countryside together. But this appears to be the Irish Genealogy Deluxe Workhorse package, so it's probably best to abandon thoughts of visiting the Dublin Writers Museum, the James Joyce Centre, the famously gorgeous Long Room Library at Trinity College, the Book of Kells, the National Museum, the Chester Beatty Museum, the General Post Office, the Kilmainham Gaol (where hundreds of those involved in the Easter Rising spent time — including my next-door neighbour's great-grandmother), the Guinness Storehouse and Brewery, the Jameson Distillery, the National Art Gallery, Museum of Modern Art, Dublin City Gallery, or the National Leprechaun Museum (why not).

I take a moment to adjust my expectations before returning to the library's front desk.

~o

There must have been a traumatic experience with microfilm in my infancy (or university), for the mere word fills me with soporific dread. As the librarian hands me my first roll of microfilm, however, she seems quite excited for me, explaining that for the majority of

Irish people of the eighteenth and nineteenth centuries, these parish registers are the only record of their existence.

"They are invaluable in establishing links between families and generations," she says with cheerful but cautious enthusiasm. "You might find all sorts of people you'd thought lost."

For the next two hours, blurry images of barely legible documents penned in indecipherable script spin across the screen until I feel I might either vomit or leave the country. Never have I wished more people lost. The records are listed by date, not by name, which means that it is necessary to read, or not-be-able-to-read, every single faded, decayed, scrawled entry.

After two hundred and forty excruciating minutes, I have not found any of the names I am looking for.

All I want to do is claw my way back to the *Jeanie Johnston* and beg Patrick to take me on another tour of that blessed ship, to hear those stories brought to *life*, for god's sake, to be able to imagine something, someone, to feel something, *anything*.

I feel my dad's hand on my arm.

"I've just finished the last of the materials we ordered. Maybe we should call it a day," he whispers.

I try not to explode with relief.

He smiles. "You look as if you could use a pint of something."

TUESDAY

10 BOW STREET

We're having lunch with a cousin today. I've never met him before. And he's not actually my cousin. He's my fifth cousin, a descendant of one of the brothers of Henry Faunt, my great-great-great-grandfather. So, when I think about it, I am probably as closely related to him as I am to Kermit the Frog.

"Well, not quite," my dad corrects me gently. "You had the same great-great-great-great-grandparents."

I pause for a moment, try to feel into the significance of that connection, the importance of it, but I get nowhere. Instead, what comes to mind is a friend who used to help settle international students into Canadian schools. Many of the Asian students wanted to adopt Anglo names upon arrival, and while my friend always encouraged them to keep their original names, she also counselled the more determined students through the renaming process, explaining why their particular choices — Cinderella, in once case; Kermit, in another — might not be the best one with which to begin school.

I share this story with my dad, who giggles and tells me that when he was a boy, he wished he had been called Margrave, the alternate name his parents had been considering for him. "I just couldn't think of a lovelier name than Margrave," he says rhapsodically. And for the nth time in my life, I wonder how it was that his coming out came as a surprise to anyone.

But it did.

My dad once told me that he might not have come out at all had his parents still been alive. It would have been too distressing for them, he had explained, as people of their generation — his father was born in 1879 — would have had such trouble understanding.

My dad was what was politely known as *an accident*, born thirteen years after his sister and a full eighteen years after his brother. His mother was a shocking forty-three years of age when she gave birth to my dad in 1936; his father was fifty-seven. During one father-son outing to the Toronto Exhibition when my dad was five or six, two ladies (as they were called in those days) noticed him being restless and energetic.

Grandfather is going to be tired, they commented.

Grandfather, nothing, my dad's dad replied. *Father is going to be tired.*

Rather than Margrave, my dad was given his father's name, Joseph, and quickly became known as Junie Joe, a nickname he hated almost as much as the perennial question, *And are you going to study law like your father when you grow up?* He adored his father but had no wish to be his clone, and he was far more interested in musical systems than legal ones. Joseph Sr. died of cancer when my dad was only ten. From then on, he was raised by his mother and maternal grandmother, both feisty, independent women for the time, famous for lively, apocryphal storytelling and strong personal opinions.

All of these details would become relevant decades after the fact, when my father found himself lying on a psychiatrist's sofa pondering the possible causes of his homosexual condition, as it was viewed in those days. *Loss of father figure at tender age* was no doubt duly noted. *Excessive feminine influence, early exposure to ideas of women's liberation, possible coddling as the only child in a household of women,* et cetera. According to the theories of the day, all of this put a man at risk of homosexual tendencies, but my father never bought into any of it. By the time he sought psychological counsel, the only question that truly plagued him was *How can I find a good man with whom to share my life?*

The psychiatrist was unable to help.

At which point, my father's brother, Dick, who had organized and paid for the psychiatric sessions, severed all ties with my father, a move that was sadder than it was surprising. The two had never been particularly close, Dick having moved out of the house and married shortly after my father was born. In essentials — politics, priorities, laughter, love, music — they were as different as two people from the same family could be, but being rejected and disowned by a brother is painful in any case. Only on his deathbed, almost twenty years after the shunning, did Dick call my father to his side. They exchanged a few words and Dick gave my dad some family papers, but by then, of course, they were family to each other only in name.

∽

My dad connected with the fifth cousin we are meeting today through a genealogy website, and Colin and his wife, Shirley, are apparently as keen on the ancestry racket as my dad. They've shared a couple of email exchanges over the last couple of months, but this is the first time they will be meeting in person.

My dad does that a lot. Tracks down and meets up with people of vague and distant relation to him. They'll meet for lunch, share family trees, look at family photographs with an eye for familiar traits and resemblances — *I think she might have my grandmother's forehead* — that sort of thing. When I call my dad and ask what he's been up to, I am not at all surprised when the response is *Oh, I rented a car and drove to [unknown woebegone hamlet] to have lunch with a third half-cousin twice-removed whom I'd never met.*

"I think you'll like Colin and Shirley," my dad assures me. "They sound quite fun."

Which does not assure me. I have been on these drives to unknown woebegone hamlets. I have lunched with these third cousins twice-removed. And while they have all been perfectly nice (no axe murderers, so far, that I can detect), Great Fun is not how I would describe any of them.

But I'm determined to be a good sport. To rise to the occasion. To bring as much joy and sunshine to this trip as I possibly can, for my father's sake. So when he adds the phrase, *Colin thinks we should meet for lunch and then spend the afternoon together at the Registry of Deeds*, I tamp down all feelings of claustrophobia and panic, suppress my urge to run to the pub and guzzle four pints of Guinness before they arrive, and manage to summon enough of my Irish ancestry to slant my vowels and say *sounds grahnd.*

CORLESS'S PUB

I'm not sure why I was expecting Colin to resemble a walrus and Shirley to arrive in a sweater set, sensible shoes, and with a small hard handbag that could be used to whack someone over the head if necessary, but they're not like that at all. They're very smiley, for one thing, lively and casual. To my great relief, they also appear to be good-humoured, which is appropriate, as Shirley's voice has the exact — but *exact* — tone, pitch, and VOLUME of Brian's mother in Monty Python's *Life of Brian*. Even the accent is the same, as Shirley hails from East London. Indeed, it would be difficult to overstate the *identical* nature of these two voices, though I'm verging on that very thing right now. (If you are unfamiliar with this voice, well, poor you, first of all, and second, you would be well served to put this down and find it on YouTube: *He's Not the Messiah — Monty Python's Life of Brian*)

All of this means that regardless of what she is saying, Shirley's every word has a comic quality to it, as if the cast of Monty Python were hovering above her like angels of inspiration, all of them dressed in sweater sets and sensible shoes and whacking each other over the head with small handbags.

The other thing is, Colin is pronounced Colon, which is a parental choice I've always found puzzling. A bit like naming your child Bladder or Large Intestine. So from the moment Colon introduces himself and Shirley looks at my father and squawks, *WELL, AREN'T YOU JUST THE VISION OF DAPPER AND DANDY!* I am already having a ball.

Within five minutes of sitting down, however, the conversation begins to sound something like this:

— So, you're descended from William Faunt.

— Yes, brother of Henry.

— WHO HAD A LONE SON, GEORGE.

— Yes, precisely. From Westmeath.

— And George's twin sons were James and Thomas.

— NO, THE TWINS WERE JAMES AND JOHN.

— Really? I thought the twins were James and Thomas.

— No, it was James and John, but John died in infancy. Thomas was the younger sibling.

— Oh, I see. And which one married into the Thompsons?

— That was Albert. Thomas had seven children, and it was . . . oh, now . . . it was . . .

— MARGARET!

— Yes, sorry, Margaret, who married Charles Moore.

— WHO WAS A BASTARD!

— Oh, was he?

— Yes, I have the birth certificate.

— Oh, do you? I'd love a copy of that.

— Yes, of course, I'll send that to you.

— AND IT WAS CHARLES'S SON SPENCER WHO WAS HIS GREAT-GRANDFATHER.

— Whose great-grandfather?

— COLON'S.

— On my mother's side.

— Oh, I see.

[*a clearing of throats*]

— Well, isn't this fascinating.

Thank god for Monty Python. That's all I can say. And for Guinness, which we all order pints of, in addition to sandwiches and chips.

~9

For the remainder of the lunch, I play a game with myself. I chew every mouthful of food fifty times before swallowing, and I allow myself only one swig of Guinness per fifty-times-chewed bite of food. As games go, it's not one from the barrel of laughs category, but it keeps me going. And it keeps the beer from disappearing too quickly. We still have a full afternoon in the Registry of Deeds ahead of us, so while I am tempted to sit here and get quietly sozzled while family trees are hacked apart around me, I need to be able to a) stay awake; b) read the unreadable; c) provide research assistant services of the *do not moisten a digit to aid in page turning* variety.

I keep catching the eye of a small, fragile-looking man at a table by the window. He's pale, well groomed, and looks melancholy, though every time our glances graze each other, he smiles quickly and reveals the tiniest row of teeth I've ever seen in an adult mouth. As I am chewing my egg salad sandwich the requisite fifty times, I speculate on how tooth size might affect chew-efficacy. No conclusions. As the conversation around me gets progressively more bludgeoning — "I have reason to believe that our great-great-great-grandfather's brothers were *Paul*, George, and William, not *Peter*, George, and William . . ." — I try to remain engaged, to nod occasionally, but beneath the surface I am exploding with questions about what drives this mad pursuit.

I excuse myself from the table and go in search of the wifi password, and subsequently the toilet, where I sit down and fling myself onto the internet in search of answers to the following question: why are people so obsessed with genealogy?

Actually, I type the words, *Why do people go so bat-shit crazy over genealogy?*, but the results are mixed. So I tone it down, streamline the question.

As it turns out, the condition has an actual name — progonoplexia, an obsession with ancestry, a.k.a. *ancestoritis* — and it's fast becoming an epidemic. Apparently, genealogy is now the most-visited category of websites other than pornography. And it's considered the second most-popular hobby in the United States after gardening. There are television series — *Who Do You Think You Are?* and *Genealogy Roadshow* — with large and loyal followings, genealogy books and websites galore; personal DNA tests have become all the rage, with millions of spit-in-a-jar home test kits being sold every year. Recently, a friend of mine received a DNA kit as a Christmas gift from his father, who was terrifically excited about the technology until it was revealed that he was not actually his son's, uh, father.

It is simple enough to comprehend the thirst for basic knowledge about one's roots, an understanding of who we are and who came before us, but my god, second only to *porn*? This is no idle curiosity we're witnessing. What is this massive hunger for ancestry really about?

Fortunately, there is no one waiting to use the toilet, so I am able to settle in and do a bit more investigating. Very quickly, and not surprisingly, I discover genealogical searches and family trees in the world's oldest documents and traditions. There is something called the Confucius Genealogy Compilation Committee, which has collected 2,500 years of genealogical data pertaining to Confucius. Hesiod's epic poem "Theogony" (700 BCE) traces the origins and genealogies of the Greek gods. Muslims draw Mohammed's line back through Abraham to Adam and Eve, and the Bible is full of lists of who begat whom, with a passage in Luke (3:23–38) listing the patrilineal genealogy of Jesus back through a whole whack of begats to God himself. So the tracing of patrilineal lines could be said to be as old as story. Clearly, genealogy has always mattered to people (if for no other reason than inheritance of property, wealth, title, and/or pomposity), but confirmation of greatness or entitlement doesn't seem to be what motivates most people to investigate their ancestry anymore.

So what does?

Well, no one popping up on this lavatory internet search seems to know. I find all sorts of blog posts from genealogy lovers saying some version of *we who stalk the archives and parish registries are just a nutty bunch!* but I discover nothing more penetrating than that. Some of the most notable genealogists are the Mormons, who see genealogy as nothing short of a soul-saving mission, the belief being that a person can retroactively baptize relatives who died without learning about the Mormon gospel, if armed with sufficient documentation about those 'unsaved' relations. Which is, if nothing else, fascinating logic.

My own intuitive take on the subject is that we've become so scattered and uprooted, cultural tumbleweeds, no longer gathered in the sorts of communities or tribes that are woven into land, story, art, food, song, and ancestral wisdom the way we would have been — all of us — once. And it only makes sense that if we have become separated from all that bound us to the land and people who sang us into existence that we should yearn for our biological music of origin, a connection and reunion of sorts, a wholeness we might never have consciously identified as being missing, but which answers a vague yet unrelenting ache.

Just prior to coming on this trip, a friend descended from Russian Jews told me how lucky I was, that she would love to go on a genealogical mission like this one, would love to know more about her ancestors, but waves of devastating and destructive pogroms make that impossible. *This* I have no trouble understanding: the urge to unearth buried histories, silenced pasts, severed families; the longing someone would feel to breathe such a past into existence, forgotten people to life.

What I have trouble grasping, what I'm grappling with here in the toilet stall of Corless's Pub, is not that at all, but rather the obsession, let's call it, with knowing — long after you've hammered down the basic genetic lines and geographies, all of which have already been exhaustively documented and celebrated — who your fifth cousin's great-great-great-grandfather's wife's brother was, where he was born, what his death certificate looks like, and how exactly his name was spelled. Do we know ourselves any more deeply for having this kind of information, this level of detail? If not, then what is it these people are actually looking for? Even with the help of the almighty internet and untold strings of algorithms, I'm no further ahead in understanding that human mystery than when I first sat down to tinkle, though the intersection of genealogical and gynae-cological activities at this moment does amuse me.

∾

I return to my people. No one seems to have noticed my protracted absence, nor has the conversation steered from its earlier course. There is now talk of a John Egan from Mullingar to whom we *may or may not* be related — correct me, but isn't that the case with every-one on Earth? — so I return to the fifty-chews-per-bite playoffs, the final few rounds involving crusts and soggy chips and the skillful meting out of the remaining Guinness.

Somewhere into chew thirty-two, I take note of the fact that virtually all of the genealogy-minded relatives I've met over the years have been, well, late-fall chickens, if you will. And this feels signifi-cant, this interest in our past at the point when we are so consciously facing our own mortality. Is all of this a way of immortalizing ourselves, a laying down of stones of which one's own could be the next in line? What happens when the edge of life becomes visible in the distance, when we find ourselves poised to tip into history, to be remembered as a name, a stretch of dates, a series of branches connected to those who have come before? Does ancestry begin to feel as much like the future as the past, a trans-temporal map of who we will become as much as who we have been? If so, then I suppose it does matter, doesn't it, that the headstone reads *Paul* and not *Peter*. That we knew who you were. That you are remembered.

~

"AND WHAT ABOUT YOUR SIBLINGS, JOSEPH? ARE THEY STILL WITH YOU?"

I cannot remember what number chew I'm on when this question is asked, but I cut it short and swallow. Take a long swig.

"My brother died twenty years ago, but my sister's still alive," my dad replies. "She'll be ninety-three in a few months."

"OH, I'M SORRY ABOUT YOUR BROTHER. BUT HOW LOVELY TO HAVE YOUR SISTER STILL KNOCKING ABOUT!" is Shirley's tactless yet endearing reply.

My father barks out a strange laugh, a flat sound such as the one he might emit were he to be whacked on the back with a canoe paddle. Then he smiles and changes the subject. Asks Colon something about the whereabouts of certain family members just prior to the Great Famine. To which Colon says something about a great-great-uncle — or was it a great-great-great-uncle? — and I go back to my chew-counting. And to thinking about my father's sister.

Dot and my dad were as close as two siblings could be, their differences both legion and irrelevant. When I was growing up, our families shared time, vacations, days on the beach, evenings on the front porch, songs around the piano, and endless games and laughter. The children of one family would happily spend time in the home of the other, political discussions were set aside for the sake of higher enjoyment, and my dad and Dot amused and loved each other, pure and simple.

So when my father came out to Dot and she stood up from the table and made the decision *not to see him anymore* (and meant it — it's been more than forty years and she's as resolute as ever), it was beyond saddening and surprising: it was devastating. An amputation. It meant that stepping into the truth about himself cost my father the entirety of his immediate family: connections with both of his siblings; his marriage to my mother, a woman he adored (still does); and day-to-day home life with his children.

And I may be entirely off the mark about this, lost in pop-psych conjecture of the worst kind, but I have wondered, at times, if that very severing from his family in everyday life might have in some way fuelled my father's obsession to connect to family elsewhere. In distant cousins and archives, in family trees and old photographs. In woebegone hamlets within driving distance of Toronto.

In this pub in central Dublin.

THE REGISTRY OF DEEDS

"This is the oldest Georgian street in all of dear, auld, dirty Dublin," Colon tells us good-naturedly, as we turn onto the sidewalks of Henrietta Street. "It dates back to 1720."

The short, wide cobblestone street is flanked by contiguous brick houses and it isn't dirty at all, though the brick itself is a dark reddish-brown. The houses are plain, unadorned, but the entrances are colourful, with arched doorways and handsome doors painted fire engine red or forest green or the dark purple of eggplants. As with so many Georgian buildings, these are attractive but vaguely surreal, as if they were a façade, a film set, a quiet Potemkin village. There are no front gardens or lawns, for one thing, no sign of actual life, just one long brick wall with symmetrically spaced doors and windows, as if the whole thing had been a drawing exercise and any minute a giant arm might reach down from the sky and begin erasing it.

When I step back to take a photograph, a young woman walks out of the very door I am centring in my lens.

"You find this quaint, do you?" She laughs. "*Jaysus*, you should try living here!"

She is about to pull the door closed behind her when the voice of an older woman calls from inside. "Polly!" The young woman winces and rolls her eyes, ducks back inside.

As quickly as it came to life, the street draws closed again.

∽

The Registry of Deeds is the most impressive building yet, though not architecturally. It's lovely enough, with curved wooden staircases in the smaller library and ample natural light throughout, but what makes the place stunning is the collection it houses. They aren't books on the shelves so much as works of art, enormous leather-bound tomes sheathed in burlap that is torn and discoloured with age. The books are ancient, weary, as if they'd been hauled around in a rough wagon for centuries or unearthed from a crypt. The earliest volumes have the date 1708 painted on their cracked and peeling leather spines. They are gigantic in the truest sense, with proportions suitable to such a personage: two feet in length, more than a foot wide, and containing up to 600 heavy parchment pages. Impossible to hold and read, the volumes must be set down and opened on drafting-style tables in order to be perused.

At the end of the building is a room tucked away from the others. It's home to the tombstones, so named because these particular volumes are the thickest and heaviest of the lot. Bookcases have been built to house a single one horizontally on each shelf. These books are also bound in burlap, numbered 1 to 883, and shelved floor to ceiling. Ladders stand at various points around the room.

Colon points to a sign on one of the bookshelves: *Caution: Heavy Books.*

"Yes indeed, sir. Some o' dem weigh twelve or turteen kilos," warns the young man giving us our orientation tour. Which explains why he looks like a wrestler, his biceps bulging out of the sleeves of his T-shirt as he gestures around the room. It's an unusual look for a librarian. My dad's eyes widen as the man points to the upper shelves. "Be sure to exercise caution carting these volumes up and down the ladders to the upper shelves," he suggests genially. "Or appeal to the youngest and fittest among you to do the most arduous lifting."

All eyes bend in my direction.

Our brawny librarian explains that most of the volumes hold memorials of deeds — transcriptions of records such as leases, land transfers, marriage settlements — which were copied by professional scribes in the nineteenth century to create these master copies. After making some enquiries about the nature of our search, he offers a few suggestions — the *Names Index*, the *Townlands Index* — and is beginning to explain the indexing system when Shirley cuts him off and lets him know that "ACTUALLY WE'VE BEEN HERE BEFORE AND FOUND ALL SORTS OF DELIGHTFUL SURPRISES AND TODAY WE HAVE THE PLEASURE OF SHOWING THE PLACE TO OUR RELATIVES FROM CANADA."

The librarian smiles. I try to determine his knowledge of Monty Python by his facial expression, but it's hard to tell. He's either stunned — it's quite a voice even without the comedic reference point — or having the time of his life and containing himself.

"Well, I'll leave you to it then," he says, giving each of us a friendly nod. "Best of luck to you."

The door closes soundlessly behind him.

"WELL, WASN'T HE NICE?"

My dad catches my eye and winks.

Colon and Shirley decide to consult the indexes in the small library down the hall. They are looking for references to Faunt in all of the possible parishes where the family might have resided in the eighteenth and nineteenth centuries — something like that, anyway — while my dad and I go through the *Names Index* looking for any listing of Faunt or Egan or Lougheed or Thompson. My dad reminds me to check for variant spellings — Thompson with a *P* and without, et cetera — as clerical errors were as common then as now.

At which point two identical black-suited and moustachioed men in bowler hats begin striding around in my mind, as anyone familiar with the comic adventure series *Tintin* and its chronically clumsy detectives Thompson and Thomson will understand. I can just see them stumbling up and down the library's ladders, dropping books and scattering pages, while trading their trademark tautological nonsense.

We are on a Faunt-finding mission of variant spellings, if my name is Thompson!

To be precise: if my name is Thomson, there is a fount of variously spelled defunct Faunts to be found!

Smiling, I heave a large leather-bound volume labelled *1735– 1785* onto a reading shelf and open the cover carefully, delicately, immediately transfixed by the physical history I am touching. The parchment itself is mottled and crisp, the script elegant, classical. The bottom right-hand corners of the vellum pages are shiny with human oil, curled by hundreds of years of fingertips and thickened, closer to the texture of leather than paper. Some of the more damaged pages have been bandaged, the gauze flaking and pulling away, as if from a wound. I spend a long time running my fingers between and around these edges, feeling the ache and swell of centuries, enjoying the low rustle and crumpling sound each page makes as it is turned.

I get to my task eventually, but not before encountering half of the kids with whom I grew up: Brady, Burns, Carew, Connor,

Driscoll, Duncan, Findlay, Fisher, Fitzpatrick, Fogerty, Foran, Gaffney, Gallagher. It could be the attendance list of my public school in Peterborough, Ontario. Most of those families had been in Canada for generations by then, so we never thought of ourselves, or anyone else, as Irish. Yet here are our ancestors speaking their names to a scribe, who would have dipped his feather into an inkwell and inscribed it on a sheet of parchment for the record.

Which I now hold in my hand.

Over the course of the 1820–1829 volume, my entire childhood passes before my eyes: Carroll (boy I had a crush on in grade two; later jailed), Costello (first boy I ever kissed, in the dark, on a dare; still recall the hot humiliation), Donnelly (*That Catholic Family*, as my grandmother used to call them; ten kids), Downey (neighbour up the street with the golden retriever who humped all the local children), Duffy (boy I kicked in the shins for pushing me off the monkey bars, an act for which I was rewarded by my teacher with a whispered *good for you!*), Faber (round, flatulent kid who sat in front of me in Mrs. McNeill's class), Flaherty (guidance counsellor arrested for shoplifting), Garrity (math teacher with legendarily bushy eyebrows, as if rodents were sleeping on top of his glasses), Healey (sweet guy who collected stamps and had lemony B.O.). I am tumbling back in time, falling through layers of memory, stumbling into people I haven't thought about in years, decades, when — wait a minute — I turn back one page and zero in one of the names.

"Faunt!" I call out. Can't help myself. I feel heroic. "Dad, I found a Faunt!" My first pottery shard!

He's gone off somewhere. The room is empty. I stand frozen with my finger on the entry, waiting for him to reappear.

The unlikely assistant has found a Faunt, if my name is Thompson!

To be precise, if my name is Thomson, it is likely to assist if the found Faunt is a find!

My dad pushes into the room.

I leap up, flap my hands around. "I found a Faunt!"

My dad seems pleased, though not quite as thrilled as I might have hoped. He tells me to jot down the reference number on a slip of paper: 200–170.

"That'll be in the tombstone room," he tells me. "If you can pull the volume off the shelf, I'll meet you in there and we can see if it's something interesting."

Something interesting! I push into the tombstone room, locate volume 200 on an upper shelf, wheel over one of the ladders, climb up to the top shelf, extract the 600-page brute slowly, carefully, teetering it down the ladder and heaving it over to the long communal reading table.

The pages are thick, fibrous, mottled with foxing. They feel swollen with plagues and poxes, though I don't know if that's possible. Unlike the indexes, in which the script is easily legible and the organization of information relatively clear, these pages are home to sweeping calligraphy that is both stunning to behold and impossible to read, full of swirls, flourishes, and antiquated abbreviations. The language itself is legalistic, obfuscatory, beyond convoluted.

> He the S Robert Thompson at the request and appointment
> of the S Tho-s Hewit and also the S Tho-s Hewit did grant
> bargain sell assign Transferr Let over release and Confirm unto
> the S Wm Lyons his heirs exrs aom-rs and assigns all those
> two pieces or parcells of Ground Situate lying and being on
> the East side of Hercules Lane in the Town of Belfast afore-
> said each containing in length at the Front next to the S. Lane
> or Street twenty feet be the same more or less and extending
> backwards in depth respectively ninety seven feet and ninety
> nine feet or thereabouts lie the same more or less together with
> the inessuages or Tenements thereon standing and being as the
> same premes were then on the Tenure and occupation of the S

Tho-s Hewit and his Undertenants with the appure Situate in
the parish of Belfast Barony of Belfast Co of Antrim.

"Good lord . . ." I mutter when I reach the end of the sentence. A man on the opposite side of the table looks up over his reading glasses. His eyes tuck back down again before I have a chance to apologize or explain myself, and then my dad pushes into the room and joins me at the reading table. He pages through the book with his right hand, while his left jiggles wildly, flopping around like a dying fish and making a soft thumping sound on the desk. The man opposite looks up with a raised eyebrow and watches for a moment before returning to his reading.

"Here it is," my dad whispers, locating entry 170. He is speed-reading as though it were the daily newspaper, doesn't seem slowed by the language at all. While turning pages with his good hand, he fumbles with the other, his notebook whisking across the table and scissoring into the tombstone's pages, the tremor stirring the whole scene like a toddler making a mess. The man glances up from across his book again and looks annoyed. I turn my eyes into darts until he looks back down. Suggest to my dad that I take dictation. To which he nods, looking relieved.

"Indented deed of agreement bearing the date fifth of March eighteen hundred and fourteen and made between Richard Faunt of Hanstown in the County of Westmeath Esquire Captain in the Thirty-Fourth Regiment of the first part . . ." he whispers.

I write as fast as I can. Don't even try to make sense of it. I love feeling so useful, even just as a scribe.

". . . the said Richard Faunt in consideration of two hundred ninety pounds made over unto the said Thomas Faunt that part of Habsborough containing one hundred fifteen acres and also that part of Habsborough lately demised to John Faunt of Ballinea deceased containing nine acres on which a malthouse and other houses stood."

He stops.

"Well, that's quite interesting," he whispers, skimming it again.

At some point in 1820 money changed hands between Richard Faunt and somebody else over a slice of Habsborough? How is that quite interesting?

It's a matter of gathering the facts, my dad explains patiently. Fleshing out the particulars so we know who's who and what's what, what they might have owned, where they might have lived, and in what conditions.

I look at him rereading the entry, watch him, his concentration, how much all of this matters to him, really *matters*. What does it give him, this information? Why on earth does he *care*?

Shirley pushes into the quiet room. "HERE YOU ARE! WE WONDERED IF YOU'D GIVEN US THE SLIP!"

Colon trails behind saying *shush*, but Shirley takes no notice. The man opposite draws a finger across his eyebrow, returns to his reading.

"WOULD YOU LOOK AT THESE LADDERS! YOU'LL NOT FIND ME TRUNDLING UP AND DOWN! NOT WITH MY KNEES! I'M LIABLE TO TAKE A SPILL ONTO THE FLOOR AND HAVE MY SKIRTS FLY UP OVER MY FACE, AND YOU'D NONE OF YOU WANT *THAT*, BELIEVE ME!"

The man across the reading table looks up again, but this time he smirks, puts his hand to his mouth, and coughs, stifling a chuckle.

They haven't been able to find any Faunt references in the parish indexes, Colon tells us, but they have found several mentions of another line of his family, a great-great-grandfather named Farrell, who was a blacksmith. Colon believes this might explain the affinity he has always had for metalwork, particularly wrought iron.

Sorry, *what*? A distant aproned relative smashed hammers onto red-hot horseshoes and that explains why, one hundred years later, Colon appreciates metal railings? Are we all quietly losing our minds together at the Registry of Deeds or might this actually be true? Are my Faunt genes responsible for my affinity for dark ale, in that case?

After all, as we've just learned, part of Habsborough lately demised to John Faunt of Ballinea deceased did contain nine acres on which a malthouse and other houses stood. But wait, wait, what about all the people descended from blacksmiths who *don't* like metalwork? Or people who love metalwork whose ancestors were bakers? How many of the traits and characteristics of our ancestors are well and truly passed down to us, and do we get to pick and choose? What if we are descended from a long line of bigots who treated people abominably, set cats on fire, and passed on stolen booty to their heirs? What then?

Normally I'm quite a tolerant and open-minded person, more than willing to shimmy out onto the furthest branches of reason and dangle there happily, without judgment. I choose to view the world energetically, to postulate a swirl of transcendental occurrences behind life's seemingly banal events, to prefer the possibility of a celestially orchestrated synchronicity over the flipped-coin meaning-lessness of coincidence, to swim in the notion of a connectedness that is largely unseen, and to believe that what we put out, in thought and deed, has a way of boomeranging back to us. So why am I being such a wet-blanket skeptic about the possibility that Colon's apprecia-tion of wrought iron railings might have its origins in some ancestral hammering that still pulses through his blood?

I don't know, actually. I can't put my finger on it. But there is something about all of this that rankles me, deeply. The enervating language, perhaps. The persnickety detail. The gaping absence of women. The airless rooms. Whatever it is, I try to put it aside as I haul thirty-pound tomes up and down ladders, on and off reading tables, into and out of shelves, and take four or five more dictations from my father, all variations on the theme of *A Memorial of an Indenture of Conveyance bearing date the fifth day of January one thou-sand seven hundred and seventy-four made between Thomas Pilkington of Westmeath in the County of Sligo farmer of the first part and Richard Flaherty of Ballymote in the County of Sligo merchant of the second part*

and Wm Flaherty esq of Ballymote in the County of Sligo of the third part
reciting as therein is recited whereby for the conveyance therein ment.

It's a long afternoon.

We find only the one Faunt reference, but it is not particularly revelatory or helpful in answering the great question of why our ancestors left Ireland when they did, though over the course of three short days, I have already developed what I believe is a very plausible theory: All the Bloody Rain. I mention this to my dad, who emits such a forced laugh it does not fully exit his mouth.

I have also developed a partial theory about the fervour with which everyone else in the room is submerged in these documents. Namely, that there is a personality divergence at work here, a core wiring that sets people up to explore in very different ways. Because it's not just that I'm bored, it's that I don't learn this way; never have.

If I were to come to Ireland on an ancestral mission of my own, I'd be inclined to head to the library and establish the basics — County Sligo, got it — before heading back outside. From there, I'd hop a bus to the west coast and just sort of *take it all in*: the sights and smells, the textures of buildings, the feel of the land, the songs of the wind, shapes of the landscape, views (if any), the faces and stories of the surrounding people — direct descendants or not. I'd sketch the eyes of the people, their hands, boots, teeth. I'd wander and listen, meander back roads and graveyards, stare out at the sea, pay attention to my dreams. And I would come away at the end of the week with precisely nothing in the way of facts about who I was related to, how much land they farmed, who owned it, how rich anyone was, why my ancestors left, or on which boat. But I wonder if I might discover something of a collective truth of who they were.

Who knows.

More immediately, my shoulder aches. It's an old injury that flares up from overuse, so I beg off the tombstone schlepping for a bit and take a turn around the building, stopping at one of the south-facing windows and noticing for the first time a view of the city's rooftops and steeples. A flicker of sunshine. Directly below the window is a parking lot and an attendant in a fluorescent-yellow vest, a man with skin the colour of coal. It is not until my eyes rest on him that I realize he is the first man of colour I have seen since arriving in Ireland.

He strolls, patrols, wanders the lot as slowly as a human body can walk. Not quite. But he is in no hurry. None at all.

I watch for the time it takes him to amble the full length of the lot.

Which is a long time.

Long enough for me to become infinitely more fascinated in his ancestry than my own.

Where has he come from? What has him in Ireland? How long has he lived here? Who and what might he have left behind to come here? What distant, hot land shimmers in his heart as he patrols these cool, wet grounds? How does this man connect with his ancestors, the stories and people of his past? Are there any archival records of them? Any Indentures of Conveyances or officers of the second part and esquires of the third part reciting as therein is recited whereby for the conveyance therein?

The man reaches the edge of the parking lot and stands for a moment, staring at something in the distance before turning around. He tips his head back and stretches his neck, notices me in the window, and stares for a second, less, before tucking his head forward again and looking at the ground, the cars in the parking lot, his own slow steps.

I look away. Take in the bookcases around me, three hundred years of land transfers and deeds, and try to imagine the origins of this — this meticulous system of annotation, this concept of private property and its attendant documentation, this cleaving and apportioning of land, this deadening and desensitizing language. Where do oral traditions fit into this system, I wonder, the ancestry that is woven through song and story, that is held in art, strung across song-lines, resonant in rhythms, cloth, and colour? Are those things less valuable for their inherent lack of paperwork? Less reliable for their absence of documentation, less true for their dearth of legalese? Or might it be the opposite?

I'm staring into space, into questions of ownership and the segmenting of the contoured earth into squares, when the strapping librarian approaches and asks if I'd like him to open the window.

"It's quite warm today," he notes. "A wee bit close."

He leans over to raise the window, which sticks, so even with his biceps it involves some effort. As cool air begins to swim into the building, we stand together, breathing in that way fresh air instantly inspires all animals to do, and I ask him if he has any idea when people first began to see land as something that could be carved up and sold. And when did they first start writing it all down so methodically, and why in such impenetrable language?

He raises his eyebrows, does a quick glance around the room before leaning back against one of the tables and smiling.

"Well, as you ask the question . . ." he begins. "The original purpose of this registry was to create legal documentation for the great confiscation of Gaelic property by the British in the seventeenth century."

I have to cut him off right there. "Hang on hang on hang on. These records were originally created by the British to legalize the stealing of land?"

He laughs quietly. "That would be one way of putting it, yes." Leans back on the table and glances about the room. There isn't anyone around. "A great deal of land was confiscated by the British in the 1600s for the plantations. These were a type of immigration scheme, if you will, whose goal it was to establish large Protestant land-owning communities and a Protestant ruling class on Irish soil. Of course it would be impossible to list all of the seizures of Gaelic land by the British — that comprises the unhappy history of Ireland, I'm afraid — but a vast amount was taken under Cromwell and the Act of Settlement of 1652 . . ." He looks away and surveys the shelves around us. "To your question about the origins of this registry, the deeds themselves also relate to the Penal Laws, which date back to the same period. These were exceptionally harsh laws that stripped Catholics of land ownership rights, among other things . . ." he says, gesturing in a way that implies that these *other things* would take him days to list. "So, the records you see here deal almost exclusively with Protestant land-owners, the Anglo-Irish, if you will, who were, of course, a wee and wealthy minority."

I repeat that sweet, sad phrase — *a wee and wealthy minority* — and then see Shirley striding across the room waving a slip of paper. "THERE YOU ARE! WE WERE AFRAID YOU'D GONE OFF AND FOUND YOURSELF A PINT! WE'VE FOUND ANOTHER FAUNT AND NEED YOUR BRUTE STRENGTH TO PULL IT OFF THE SHELF!"

My heart does more than sink, it caves in on itself. Finding Faunt references implies the very history I do not wish to have, relations I would prefer to disown or at least ignore by doing a version of pressing my thumbs in my ears and yelling *la la la*. I've known that the Faunts were of British origin, that the famous Faunt sword was used in *overseas campaigns* for the Crown. My dad has told me all of that before. But I've always been able to pretend I'm not listening, to turn away from the bits I'd rather not see.

My aversion to genealogy might have less to do with the Boredom Factor as it does with this: I do not wish to be descended from these people. I want to come from more heroic people, kinder, innocent folk. I do not want the roots I have. I wish to be someone else.

I turn to the librarian. Thank him for his explanations.

He smiles warmly, stands up from the table. "I'm not sure I've answered your questions. But I hope I might have helped you to understand something of what it is you are consulting." Winks.

My dad apologizes when he sees me, reports the news — that they haven't found anything — and assures me this will be the last request for today.

"That's okay," I say. "I've had a break. A bit of fresh air by the window. And a chat with the librarian."

My dad looks up. "Which, the muscular one?"

"THE VERY ONE! I COULD SCARCELY PEEL HER AWAY!"

I locate and lower the requested tome from its shelf and waddle it over to the table. As my dad and Shirley look up the entry, I return a few other volumes to their shelves. The last one on the table is open, its ornate script spinning my eyes as I approach it. I try to imagine the scribe who might have penned the page, how he might have sat, or stood, what he might have worn — a wig? frilly cuffs? — and how he might have held his quill, dipped it, tapped it against the inkwell. I can hear the sound the cursive writing might have made as it scratched into the parchment. And I try to picture the Protestant settlers — some of my ancestors? — whose transactions the scribe would have been recording, people who had been given title to a piece of land which had been taken from someone else so that domination of this land, of politics, of religion, could be accomplished for a distant crown.

Of course I knew Britain had spent centuries stomping across Ireland employing the standard colonial bludgeoning, oppressing, exploiting, subjugating, confiscating, and looting that makes a country Great, but today I'm less interested in the actions of the Crown or state than I am in the individuals. The people who would have arrived here in the 1600s and 1700s, the Protestant settlers themselves. Did they know they were pawns in an imperialist game? Were they sold the idea of being loyal servants of their country, their monarch, their God, convinced they were bringing the one true religion to an island of savages? Or were they aware of anything beyond a miraculous offer of land on a distant island? Did they know or care that people had been torn from their land to make way for them, or were they callous and unfeeling, content to be brutal in their takeover? How much moral agency was there in all of this, and where is *that* recorded?

I am wondering all of this in the abstract, but of course what I'm really asking is: Who were these people and can I bear to be descended from them? And if I *am* descended from them, what does that say about me?

~

"WELL, WE MAY NOT HAVE FOUND MUCH, BUT WE CERTAINLY HAD A GOOD TIME!" Shirley declares as we're descending the staircases to the exit.

"Actually, it may be good news not to have found anything. The librarian was explaining that many of those early records from the seventeenth and eighteenth centuries were just the Crown's way of creating legal titles to land they'd confiscated from the Irish," I say. "So I'd rather not be related to anyone in that library anyway."

There is a heavy silence. The sound of scuffing on the steps. My dad says nothing. He is looking down, watching his feet. I can tell he's annoyed by my comment.

Even I'm annoyed by my comment. It was callous, naive. Why do I say things like that? What gets into me? It's as if I believe that by feeling guilty I will absolve myself of guilt. That denying my heritage will make it disappear. But I know (don't I?) that the opposite is true: that what we push away pulls at us, that denial festers, aggravating the very thing it attempts to hide.

Eventually, Colon mumbles something about the importance of historical context, that one must be careful not to judge the actions of the past with the sensibilities of the present, recalling the history that predates these records, the Norman Invasion in the twelfth century, for instance, even the Viking invasions of Ireland in the eighth century. "It's not as if the Protestant settlers of the seventeenth century were disturbing an idyll," he offers.

"Yes, maybe it's more complicated . . ." I say, trying to poultice the wound I've cut into the afternoon. "I suppose I'm just trying to look on the bright side of not finding anything conclusive today."

My dad and Colon mumble vague agreement.

We gather our things from the lockers, sign out of the building, push outside. I give my temples a little massage, squeeze and stretch my eyes, let the images of those documents, all that loopy script, drain from my mind.

And only when I tip my head back and take in a breath of the sky do I realize that it would have been these same sorts of documents that tore Indigenous homelands into strips and parcelled them out to settlers in what would become known as Canada. It would have been this same tangled language used to obfuscate, subjugate, and create documents designed to annihilate existing nations and clear the way for settlements, railways, mass deforestation, mining, a vision of the Earth as a supply of resources to be exploited; duplicitous documents that were based on the concept of private property and presented to people for whom land was inviolable, part of a matrix connecting all beings, all life, water, spirit, air, and sky; documents that took all that was inalienable and sacred and declared it alien and profane; documents of dominion and possession that were contorted to confuse, couched to deceive, composed of whorls of black script, kaleidoscopic contortions of language, manipulations of belief, and calculated, cavernous promises that were broken the moment they were made. And then again and again and again, continually, ceaselessly, over centuries.

The more I look into all of this, the less I wish to find any part of myself here at all.

~9

THE ELBOWROOM

I've sought out this *health and wellness studio* in north Dublin with the intention of doing a yoga class, to stretch and breathe my way into a better state of mind after a day of genealogical contortions, but I must have misread the schedule.

"It's Zumba tonight," the woman at the registration desk says with an apologetic lean in her voice. "Yoga's tomorrow and Saturday."

I've never done Zumba before, but I believe it's a kind of Latin dance.

"Okay, I'll try the Zumba class."

The woman's eyes widen. "Have you done Zumba before then?" she asks, giving me the once-over discreetly enough that I wouldn't notice she was giving me the once-over.

I shake my head and place a ten euro note on the counter.

~9

I am wrapped in a scarf, waiting, alongside a dozen other women, for the class to begin. They are all at least a decade younger than I am, bouncy, aerobics-y, with thick mascara and tight, shiny outfits. I am beginning to wonder if I should have just joined everyone for dinner. When the Registry of Deeds closed, at last, at 4:30, Shirley and Colon proposed meeting up later to discuss our findings (or lack thereof) over a meal, but I felt myself scrambling for an alternative.

"Oh, I have a yoga class," I said, as though I didn't have a choice. As though there were a mandatory yoga class for all female Canadian tourists to Dublin and there was nothing, just nothing, I could do about it.

"WELL, AREN'T YOU DISCIPLINED! YOU'D NOT CATCH ME DOING YOGA ON MY HOLIDAY! YOU'D NOT CATCH ME DOING YOGA AT ANY TIME OF THE YEAR, FOR THAT MATTER! I SHOULD, THOUGH, SHOULDN'T I? IT'S QUITE A GOOD THING, YOGA, ISN'T IT? VERY RELAXING, THAT'S WHAT PEOPLE SAY. BUT THAT'S WHAT A CUPPA TEA'S FOR, ISN'T IT? OR THE PUB . . ."

The instructor arrives. Actually, she does more than that. She plunges through the door like a supernova sparking energy and whipped-up enthusiasm. Instantly, the pitch of the room rises by an octave, jackets are unzipped and left at the edges of the room, women spread themselves out in rows and begin bouncing on their toes, shaking their arms. I join them at the back. As far back as I can get without hanging myself on one of the coat hooks.

The next hour is one of the most exhilarating and farcical I've had in recent memory. I cannot, for one, remember when I have swung my legs in as many directions, taken as many steps and turns, shaken as many parts of my body, jumped or humped the air more. The music is loud, Latin, and over-the-top, rife with horns, hormones, throbbing rhythms, and unapologetic joy. The

instructor is electric. Infectiously playful. At one point, I am laughing so hard I have to stop and catch my breath. And then it's over.
I'm drenched, euphoric.

On the way back to the flat, I let drizzle cool my head, splatter against
my face, my teeth. I'm still laughing, bubbling over with remnant
glee, when I reach Smithfield. The square is dark and deserted, just
the odd couple sauntering across with their jackets pulled up around
their necks and an old man huddled under an umbrella. His gait is so
familiar it stings. To see him out like this, alone, at night, in the rain.
He looks so much more vulnerable than he used to, than I'm used to.

"Dad!"

He turns, smiles. "Hi! How was your yoga class?"

I tell him all about the mix-up with Zumba, the zaniness of it all.

"Do you think I might like it?" he asks, his voice cracking a bit, as
it does these days when he's tired.

He means it. I can hear it in the tone of his question, the sincerity
it holds. My heart nearly tumbles out of my ribcage.

"Oh, Dad! I'm not sure it's your thing. I was the oldest person in
the class . . ."

"Oh, well then, forget it!" He laughs. "But maybe we could find
something fun to do together, so you're not too bored with all the
genealogy . . ."

I pull out my key and let us into our building.

"Don't worry! Just being here with you is fun . . . But what are
you doing walking around at night in the rain? Why didn't you get a
cab?" I've never fussed over my dad like this in my life. He's been all
over the world and I've never given his comings and goings a second
thought.

"A cab?! We were just at a restaurant on the other side of the
square! Shirley wanted to make sure I got home all right, but I told
her I may be old, but I'm not *that* old!"

The moment we are in the flat, he sets up on the kitchen table
and reviews his notes, checking all of the transcribing I did at the

Registry this afternoon and looking a few things up on his computer. I sit across from him and pull out my journal. I'm about to add to my list — *The Way He's Game for Anything, even Zumba!* — but I am too busy watching how much his chin is trembling, the way the tremor in his arm is sending his hand spinning in large circles above the table.

It's so strange, this disease, the way it nags and tugs at him, stirs and whirls him, demands constant, constant motion. I watch for another moment, feel myself welling up.

And then I have a brainwave.

Movement of all kinds is known to be helpful for people with Parkinson's, but movement *to music* can apparently have a particularly transformative effect, I read recently. I reach for my phone and find the article within seconds. While dancing, it says, people's tremors can lessen significantly, their stiffness and balance dramatically improve. "When I'm dancing, I don't have Parkinson's anymore," reported a man whose gait had become rigid and laboured and whose tremors encompassed his entire body. The complexities of the illness, and of the brain itself, combined with the mysteries of music and its effects on the brain, mean that it isn't entirely clear why dancing can be so miraculous, only that it can be.

I look up and watch my dad again. Look down and search *Dancing Parkinson's Dublin.*

And sure enough, there is an organization called Move 4 Parkinson's offering Dancing Well classes on Friday mornings.

It's perfect.

My dad has always loved to dance. In his own very particular way. When we were kids, his moves used to send my brothers and me into hysterics. He loved to show us how hip and with-it he was by doing something he called *rock dance*, a display which included the wild flailing of arms, a series of strange boxing moves, and a clicking sound he made in one cheek. It was funny when he danced for the family in private but embarrassing in the company of friends (who would stand wide-eyed and stupefied) and downright mortifying when he became inspired in public places: sidewalks (many, many times), subway platforms (less often, only because we would threaten to push him, or ourselves, onto the tracks), bookstores, public buildings, restaurants playing danceable music, et cetera.

As we got older, the embarrassment morphed into delight, and my brothers and I have all been known to lapse into versions of 'rock dance' to the horror of our own children. For my fortieth birthday, some friends hosted a giant dance party in their barn and my dad spent much of the evening tearing up the floor with anyone willing to oblige him. He knew he was being ridiculous but seemed enchanted by the laughter he was inspiring. Of the many comments I received after the party, the simple phrase *And, oh my god, your dad's dancing* . . . was by far the most common.

> *Hello, I am visiting Dublin from Canada with my father, who has Parkinson's. He is very active and enjoys dancing. We are only here for another week, but would it be possible to attend the Dancing Well class this coming Friday? Thanks so much.*

I am about to share my idea but stop myself. He looks busy, focused on what he's doing. I decide to wait until I've heard back from them, but already I am delighting in the image of us dancing together in Dublin.

In the meantime, I retreat to my bedroom with one of the reference books my dad has brought with him to try to bone up on my Irish history. The book, which does not waste any energy on a cleverly original title, is called *Ireland*, and according to the dust jacket, it remains one of the finest accounts of Irish history, despite its having been published first in 1839.

Chapter One: External Appearance of Ireland.
Misery of Its Inhabitants.

Ireland, by a fatal destiny, has been thrown into the ocean near
England, to which it seems linked by the same bonds that unite
the slave to the master.

The writing is melodious, poetic, which is what allows me to
get through accounts of the innumerable confiscations of land the
brawny librarian spoke about without hurling the book across the
room. Proclamations under Elizabeth I, for example, offered Gaelic
lands to anyone in England who would take them, on condition that
not a single farmer or labourer of Irish birth should be employed, thus forc-
ing the former inhabitants of those lands to take shelter in forests
and on the sides of mountains.

The subsequent wave of confiscations made sure to include
forests and the sides of mountains.

Further confiscations took place in the early 1600s under James
I and appear to have been carried out just as the librarian described.

To accomplish this enterprise, he took with him judges and
soldiers, the first to falsify the law, the second to violate it.
Both agents admirably answered his expectations. The lawyers
suddenly discovered that all the grants made by preceding
kings to the actual proprietors or their ancestors were null and
void, and that [there were] no lawful proprietors but the king.

It is unrelentingly infuriating reading, especially the Penal Laws
(passed between 1689 and 1714), which removed every manner of
right and privilege from the Catholics, as well as from any Protestant
dissenters (i.e., Presbyterians) who veered from complete submission
to the Anglican Church, the so-called Church of Ireland. There are
too many to copy out, so I jot down only the most notable examples:

— Catholics could not vote
— Catholics could not buy land

— Catholics could not teach children

— Catholics could not attend university

— Catholics could not hold public office

— Catholics could not be the guardian of a child (*Even in the hour of death, the unhappy Irish Catholic was assailed with fresh peril and terrible disgrace. He could not entrust his wife or his friend with the guardianship of his children — his choice would be null, and the wardship would lapse to the chancellor of Ireland, who had the privilege of naming Protestant guardians to Catholic minors.*)

— Catholics could not own a horse worth more than five pounds sterling (it implied a superiority to Protestant horse owners)

— Catholics could not be given, sold, or bequeathed land by a Protestant

— All land owned by a Catholic had to be equally divided among his sons, unless one son was a Protestant, in which case he got it all

— All priests had to be registered; all bishops were exiled

— Catholic churches could have neither bells nor steeples

— When allowed, Catholic churches could be built from wood, not stone, and only away from main roads

— Catholics were not allowed to educate their children in Gaelic (thus inadvertently birthing "hedge schools" — literally outside by the hedge — where the practice of education in the Irish language was carried on surreptitiously)

As the Irish political philosopher Edmund Burke put it, the laws were *as well fitted for the oppression, impoverishment, and degradation of a people as ever proceeded from the perverted ingenuity of man.*

Some of the laws began to be repealed in the late 1700s, but most were in place until 1829 and some right up to the separation of Ireland in 1920.

I lean back and stare at the ceiling for a very long time. Never did I imagine that I would wish to be Catholic, but I find myself entertaining this strange thought, though retroactively. I hope that the ancestors my father is seeking do not turn out to be people of perverted Protestant privilege, people who confiscated land or lorded over tenants or ate well while others starved. It would be so much easier, from an ethical standpoint, to descend from a long line of heroic underdogs: hardworking, oppressed people who farmed and fought tyranny, clung to the honourable side of every moral argument and always did the noble thing. It's cowardly, I grant you, but I find myself hoping for all kinds of dead ends, relations who were never registered and cannot be found because they were decent, hardworking folk who didn't abuse power or steal anything from anyone.

Which is pointless.

Because the same story just repeats itself, cartwheeling across time to whatever parcel of land our Irish ancestors — Protestant or Catholic, rich or poor — would have been "given" when they landed in Canada. Land that was carved up into a grid and sold, square by square, to be almost completely deforested, exploited, dammed, and farmed by European settlers, while Indigenous people were starved, forced onto reserves, and subjected to a relentless genocide.

It would be so much simpler to just see my ancestors as belea-guered, hard-working immigrants who knew nothing of the harm they were causing and leave it at that. But what do I really know about them? I've stared into the eyes of the portraits hanging in my father's hallway: unsmiling men in dark woolen suits and dour women in high-necked blouses and long skirts, their faces imply-ing lives wholly unacquainted with joy. Lives composed of work, religion, obligation, austerity, and duty. Lives I cannot relate to at all, that I do not wish to relate to at all. Yet to whom I am related. However distantly, I have come through those people. So who are they? And who does that make me?

I've spent much of my life turning away from my own history, ashamed to be tied to a legacy of colonialism which disgusts and privileges me, sickens and empowers me. For a long time, I tried to run from it by travelling around the world and reinventing myself, costuming myself in other languages, the fabrics and customs of other cultures, fictional identities I created for myself. When I was young, I even warped my maternal grandfather's stories about his childhood in the Canadian north into a brief belief that there was Indigenous blood in me, somewhere, that I wasn't all bad, not entirely descended from people responsible for land theft, genocide, the rapacious ravaging of the Earth. But the truth is my grandfather would wake up to dozens of Cree sleeping in part of his house, not because they were his people but because his father was a minister, his mother a woman of an apparently generous heart, and they opened their home as a refuge to anyone who had nowhere to go, fed people who were hungry. But, of course, the Cree were starving and had nowhere to go because immigrants like my great-grandparents had taken over their homeland, were benefitting from the very policies that were bludgeoning First Nations' entire ways of life. The paradox gnawed at me for years, decades. It became a portal to self-loathing, one of many. So I chose not to remember. And for a long time, I could not even have told you the names of those people, my great-grandparents.

For a while, that forgetting felt like absolution.

One of my grandfather's favourite stories involved his mother and a train trip. The family had moved south by then, to a town near Toronto, and his mother was travelling north, for a meeting of the Women's Auxiliary, I believe, her train due to stop, briefly, in the town where the family had lived. Somehow, word of her travels preceded her, and when the train stopped, the platform was *full of Indians*, as my grandfather would tell the story. *They heard Mother was going to be coming through on the train and they all came out to see her,* he would say proudly, closing his eyes and recollecting the scene. Apparently, the other ladies on the train were appalled, not only that his mother got off the train, but that she greeted everyone so affectionately — *holding hands and so forth* — and stayed out on the platform visiting until the train whistle blew. *Those women and their damn pride*, he would mutter angrily. *Mother was the only true Christian on that train.*

That last sentence always made my skin crawl; the whole story did, actually. But I loved my grandfather's telling of it, the way his face would grow thick with wrinkles as he smiled, his blind eyes lost under folds of weathered skin as he recalled his mother, her gently defiant heart.

Beyond this, I still know almost nothing about my mother's ancestry, apart from it being multi-generation Canadian of humble (probably mostly) British origins. And apart from exhaustive lists of names and dates, I also know surprisingly little of the details of my father's family. My dad's father was born in Liverpool and became a judge, I know, and his mother was Irish and independently wealthy, but I never met either of them, and my efforts at denial have left me almost entirely empty of stories.

~⃝

I lay *Ireland* down on the bed and head back to the living room, where I find my dad watching the latest episode of the Republican primaries.

"How's it looking?" I ask.

"*WUUUUUH!* The Republican Party is about to implode! They've given their delegates a choice between death by drowning, being burned alive, or having their testicles fed to an alligator." My dad whoops again and slaps his forehead. "And they're choosing the latter!"

I sit on the arm of his chair. Watch the coverage until I feel nauseous (twenty seconds) and then ask, "So, what were your parents' immigration stories, Dad?"

It shocks me that I've never asked that question before. I suppose I always thought I knew. Knew enough.

"Well, let's see . . ." He straightens up and looks at the ceiling. "My dad's family emigrated in 1893, when he was thirteen. His father — my grandfather — had worked on the railway in Liverpool, so it was probably a fairly steady job but pretty dead-end. Apparently, it was my grandmother who thought the family would be better off in Canada, so she really lit the fire. I gather she was quite a letter writer and had been corresponding with relatives who already lived in Ontario."

Already I'm surprised. His grandfather worked on the railway? Why did I think he was some well-heeled toff? I say this in kinder terms to my dad, who shakes his head.

"No-no, no-no, the English side of the family were all solidly working class."

News to me. "So where did they go?" I ask.

My dad looks buoyant, thrilled at my curiosity. He even turns away from the primaries.

"North of Toronto, near Barrie. My dad's father worked on a farm until he saved enough money to buy some land, but he didn't pay much for it. A few years ago, I talked to the people who live there now and they told me it's full of rocks. I never met those grandparents, by the way. As you know, I was born when my father was fifty-seven, and both his parents had already died."

He shifts in his seat, squints a bit. I can see him feathering back through time. "My dad was expected to help his father on the farm until he was of age, which meant twenty-one, but he hated farming, so when he got the chance he decided to go back to school. He'd only had six years of schooling in England before he emigrated, which would have been standard for working-class kids, so gradually he got his high school diploma and then went to McMaster University back when it was still on Bloor Street in Toronto. I've told you that he used to teach literacy in lumber camps in the summers, haven't I? He seemed to really love that . . ." He tilts his face up and smiles.

I can't get over what a relief this is — the railway, the farm work, the rocky soil, the lumber camps. I'd assumed we were descended from a long line of pomp and circumstance, though I grew up in a typical suburban home, my parents drove a terminally collapsing car, and we never seemed to be able to afford the things we bought. Still, I'd always envisioned his predecessors as a collection of stuffy aristocrats, so my internal compass is now spinning, ditching insufferable imaginary relations at every point on the dial and establishing new coordinates.

"And your mother? When did she emigrate from Ireland?"

My father looks perplexed. "What do you mean, when did *she* leave Ireland? This is what we've been looking into all day."

"Oh, right, of course," I say quickly, rushing to cover my gaffe.

"My mother was born on a farm just outside Strathroy, near London, Ontario. Her father died when she was three and her sister was just a baby. Her mother wasn't even thirty, but there was an unmarried aunt — with polio, I think; well, I'm not sure about that but she was in a wheelchair, anyway — and she had some money and moved in with them. My grandmother didn't get a job, but instead she started buying and selling houses in Strathroy and she did quite well at that. Women didn't have the vote in those days *unless* they owned property, in which case they could vote municipally, and I've actually gone back and found my grandmother's name on a couple of voting lists. She lived with us when I was growing up, I'm sure I've told you, so I got to know her quite well. She was a wonderful storyteller and the stories seemed to get more elaborate as time went on. I've often thought the two of you had a lot in common . . ."

He turns for a moment to listen to something the most repugnant of the candidates is saying.

"There has always been a place in politics for blowhards," he says before pressing mute. "But I don't understand how they've made room for such a revolting, asinine one. I don't understand how he's even in the running! Anyway, getting back to your question about my mother's family, they came over from Ireland in the 1830s, so just *before* the Great Famine, which has always puzzled me a bit, why they left just then. I know that two of the men, Henry Faunt and Thomas Thompson, had served as army officers."

"British army officers."

"Yes, but low-ranking ones. In those days, officers had to either purchase their commissions or have some connection to aristocracy, but in both cases that seems to have been very distant. In any case, their pensions were meagre and the British government must have wanted to rid themselves of the expense because they were offering officers a deal: if they gave up their pensions, they got two hundred acres of land in Upper Canada, which was *vast* compared to what they would have had in Ireland."

"And they'd starved and pushed Indigenous peoples onto reserves by then," I say, "so the land was free for the taking."

My dad pauses.

This is tender territory.

He subscribes to the Great Fathers of Confederation version of Canada: brave voyageurs, rugged fur-traders, hard-working immigrants, and honourable intellectuals all building a democratic new country from a *tabula rasa*. And somewhere in there, Indigenous peoples who signed treaties and gradually became part of a Just Society. One of the worst arguments of our lives began with my challenging said Happy Picture of Canada and referencing the racist government acts and policies overtly designed to decimate Indigenous peoples and their cultures, the kidnapping and abuse of generations of their children, the flagrant abrogation of treaties and agreements, and the irreversible ecological devastation that the Great Nation of Canada has ravaged upon the land since the earliest explorers saw their first beaver and thought, *Gosh, we could make a fortune if we turned those into hats.* But I believe the argument truly soured when I made reference to our ancestors having *stolen* land on which to farm.

Our ancestors were granted land, my dad had corrected me, angrily, *after leaving everything they had behind!* There was such frustration in his voice as he spoke, such pain, but I remember being coolly unfazed. I was in my early twenties at the time, knew everything, and existed in a defiant, if dubious, dwelling on the moral high ground.

It's always easy to be morally impeccable in hindsight, I remember him saying. Exasperated. *But you have no way of knowing the experience of people with limited prospects who were being offered the chance at a new life.*

I didn't have much of a rebuttal to that, as I recall, though no doubt I shrugged self-righteously.

~

Tonight I'm more subdued. Perhaps it's age. Enough time spent on the moral high ground to know it as a narcissistic hideout for the craven. Also, I refuse to spend the priceless time my dad and I have together picking a fight.

"So, they were given two hundred acres in Upper Canada in exchange for giving up their army pensions . . ." I repeat.

"Yes, yes, and the scheme was apparently a disaster, because most of the retired officers weren't very suited to pioneering life," he continues. "But one of our ancestors managed to make quite a go of it, despite a catastrophic beginning. Thomas Thompson's wife, Isabella, died of cholera about the same time they reached Quebec, and they had ten children, most of whom had come with them to Canada. Thompson was about fifty-eight at the time, so he would have been very dependent on his sons to do the heavy lifting when it came to clearing his two hundred acres of land for farming. Actually, all four families on my mother's side became farmers in Strathroy.

That's where they all met. And that's where my mother was born."
He pauses. Smiles. "You would have liked her." He stands up. "But
I'm probably boring you," he says, waving a hand.

"No, not at all."

"Well, that's progress!" He laughs. He reaches out and squeezes
my arm. "Isn't this fun?" he says before heading down the hallway.

As he passes me, I breathe in his familiar sherry-bread scent, so
soothing to me as a child, so reassuring. Even now, I am struck by
how much the fragrance of my father still comforts me, how it softens my inner world.

I listen to the bathroom door click closed and sit for a moment,
staring into the space he has left, savouring him.

Eventually, I get up and walk over to the large living room
window overlooking the street. I look out at the rooftops, the street
lamps, the light rain, and then I stare until my eyes blur. Until I
can begin to picture children losing their mother to cholera after a
six-week journey in a rank and overcrowded ship; a woman watching her husband in a dead-end job on the railway in Liverpool and
dreaming of a better life for her sons; a feisty widow buying
and selling houses, voting in municipal elections and having power
when few other women did. And I feel a vague righting, a tuning of
sorts, as these stories shift and settle within me. Faint familial songs
whose echoes I have always ignored.

∽

Back in Canada, more than a year after this Irish sojourn and inspired by it, I grew curious about my maternal grandfather's parents, the minister and his wife who had lived among the Cree in northern Ontario. I wanted to know their names, to learn a bit of who they were, to draw their stories into my own. Within seconds of blithely trawling the internet, I found confirmation that Percy Renaud Soanes had been an Anglican minister in Chapleau, Ontario. But then I snagged on something horrific: evidence that he had also been principal of St. John's Indian Residential School from 1909 to 1912.

I felt as if I'd caught fire.

I clamped my hands to my mouth, pulled my knees to my chest, curled up in my chair, stared.

The school's inaugural principal, a Reverend Duke, had stayed only a year. Under his watch, seven of thirty-one students died, most probably from a combination of malnutrition, tuberculosis, foul conditions, and heartbreak. There were no deaths during Reverend Soanes's subsequent tenure of three years, and no testimonies of sexual abuse have been reported for that school, but it was still the classic atrocity: students separated from their families, housed in appalling conditions, "civilized and Christianized," forbidden from speaking their languages, harshly punished.

I reached over and slammed the computer screen shut.

Stared at the ghost of that glow.

Tried to un-see.

And decided never to tell anyone, ever.

I was living in Vancouver at the time, steps from the ocean, so I thundered down hundreds of wooden stairs and spent the rest of the day listening to the ocean and the shushing of stones being stroked by the tide, letting the resonance of everything I had just learned toll through me. Within a few hours, I knew that for all its ugliness, I couldn't bury it, hide it, un-find what I had discovered. I needed to look the truth in the eye and let it out. Offer it up to the collective dirge. And inasmuch as I wanted to disown this, distance myself, tell no one, ever, I actually needed to stand up and speak this part of history, my history, the history of this country. Keeping it quiet would only serve my own shame.

~o

No one else in my family knew either. It seems those things weren't talked about, and by the time my mother was born, her grandfather was a minister in Toronto.

"But was he severe or authoritarian?" I asked. "What kind of person was he?"

My mother let out a breath and shook her head. "No. He was the opposite. He was kind of awkward, actually, and very kind. He was the kind of person everyone liked being around."

But who knows.

Who knows what was done in the name of God, civilization, assimilation. Regardless, this knowledge has coloured everything now. And it feels apposite, that it should do that, seep through memories, families, generations, despoiling and corroding other-wise simple histories, otherwise innocent lives. For such is the impact of such places.

WEDNESDAY

IO BOW STREET

Wrecked my shoulder doing genealogy, I tell my partner, Jay, in an email. *Either that or Zumba. Otherwise, all is GRAND. Love x 2.*

I'm not big on communication while I'm travelling. I try to do the basics — *Arrived! Fine! Still fine!* — but I don't like to play the psychic Twister game that technology has fostered. I'm so thankful I came of age when it was still possible to be on the other side of the world and actually be on the other side of the world: immersed, independent, incommunicado. Then, contact with home would involve months of anticipation, prolonged longing, the travelling of vast distances to line up at foreign post offices, gulping clutching twisting hoping hoping hoping that the *poste restante* address given to loved ones months before had been a reliable one, that mail would actually have been collected and set aside, handfuls of tissue-papery envelopes that would be passed through the bars of a wicket, letters that would be torn open and devoured on the nearest bench or patch of floor, words that were water to the parched, bread

to the famished, balm to a soul torn open by solitude, loneliness,
and an ache for words so powerful they would never taste quite the
same way again.

I also loved the physicality of the letters themselves, the palpa-
ble existence of them held to the face and smelled. For there is
something wonderful about words set down by the dancing hand,
something substantial about ink, something solid about a medium
that requires forethought, words that cannot be erased and rewrit-
ten, deleted, edited, or otherwise regurgitated but which must be
composed before they are written. There is something intimate
about pages that are leaned upon, touched, folded; something exhilarating about envelopes that are licked, bundled up and sent across
seas, packed into sacks, flung onto trains, and unpacked in rooms
that rattle with a different frequency of human electricity and song.

That said, I haven't written a real letter for years.

Still, I love that I decided not to fork out for a travel plan on my
cell phone. I love that I am restricted to wifi access and that there
has been no public internet in any of the places where we are spending our days. I love that I cannot connect to everything, everyone,
everywhere, all the time, and I hadn't noticed just how used to that
I'd become. How many times I've caught myself twitching, reaching
to check . . . to see if . . . to report . . . and being forced, instead, to
look up, around, to settle in, wonder, just to be here, in Ireland, with
my dad.

Who is currently checking his email.

∽

We will be spending today at the Royal Irish Academy. "Your great-
great-great-great-grandfather was a member of the Academy," my
dad tells me, as a way of trying to connect me to the place. But the
words *Royal Irish* trouble me a bit. They have the ring of people on
the wrong side of history again, agents for the oppressive English

regime, slum landlords, wealthy Anglos on confiscated Gaelic land, that sort of thing.

"That's not it at all," my dad corrects me. "It was a body of scholars, people who were researching various aspects of the sciences and humanities. Thomas Egan would have been a member because of his medical research, but the library is most famous for its collection of Irish manuscripts and the promotion of Irish language, culture, and literature," he assures me, before asking me to check the Academy's opening hours and wondering if there is a bit more coffee.

We have been trying to get out the door early every morning and to arrive at these places when they open, generally at 9:30. In three mornings, we have yet to manage it. We wake up in good time, but my dad is not someone who eats breakfast, rather he *enjoys* it. This morning: a poached egg with raw sheep's milk cheese on Irish soda bread, plus coffee, which I make rounds and rounds of in the tiny espresso maker so a cup can be sipped while reading a couple of online newspapers — the presumptive GOP nominee is, indeed, the testicle-eating alligator my dad predicted last night — and a second cup can be sipped while checking and answering email, scrolling through Facebook, checking yesterday's research notes, looking a few things up, and then, OH MY GOD, WE HAVE TO GO!

It's as though time hadn't been fully operational while he dipped corners of crumbly soda bread into the gooey yolk and placed a pinch of sharp cheese on top. Irish time stayed suspended during all of the subsequent sipping and scrolling — "the forest fires in Alberta have made the front page of the *New York Times* again; I guess they report on Canada when there's a chance we'll go up in smoke" — and the hands on the wall clock remained static throughout the email reading and responding, the scrolling down and down through the Facebook newsfeed — "it looks as though Char is out of the hospital" — and remained fixed during the reviewing and checking of notes and numbers of periodicals and possible leads, until suddenly, without warning, the clock snaps back into action and oh shit we need to leave right away clatter clatter scurry scurry toothbrushing toilet-flushing coat keys briefcase out the door and paddle paddle paddle all the way across town as though we're rushing to catch a train.

I get a kick out of it every morning.

It used to drive my mother up the wall. She would be standing at the door with three young children dressed, packed, and ready to go, the train about to leave, concert about to start, whatever it was . . . and my father would be upstairs, shaving perhaps, or packing, or sorting through papers, trying to find his wallet until — scurry scurry stress stress rush speed shit c'mon c'mon run — we'd arrive late, miss the train, the appointment, the first half of the play, the concert, whatever it was. And my mother, one of the most patient and forgiving people I have ever known, would be left to calm three upset children and (silently but irately) curse my father, upon whom she was infuriatingly dependent.

"He was even late for his own divorce," she told me once, decades after the fact. "It should have happened years before it did, but he kept stalling, couldn't find a way to tell me what was going on, and okay, I can understand that to a point, but how could I not be furious when I realized that half of our friends knew he was gay before I did? Can you imagine how humiliating that was?"

I asked my dad about it once, why it took him so long to tell my mother, why he never actually got around to telling her at all, how it was that she had discovered a letter he was composing to a lover named Tom, and how she had had to be the one to confront my dad with the truth about his secret life, not the other way around.

"I was so terrified that that conversation would be our last," he told me in that Paris hotel room, thirty years ago, over pastry dustings and tears. "I was so worried that I'd become estranged from her, from all of you kids. It was unfair not to tell her sooner, but I guess I wasn't ready for the possibility that I might lose all of you. Because that's what happens to a lot of gay husbands and fathers . . ." He looked out the window, wiped his eyes. "When you know you are going to cause the people you love so much pain, there never seems to be a *right time* to do it. So I guess I just kept putting it off. My family is so important to me, yet I had to hurt everyone in it . . ."

I have no idea what I said to that, if anything. I just remember the feeling of being drained. Of tears, anger, blame, false courage. I remember his asking if I had any more questions, any at all, because they were all important. And I remember that I had a few more and that we talked and cried in our pyjamas until well after noon, when we finally got dressed and headed outside, the cool air a poultice against my face, my swollen eyes, as I walked arm in arm through Paris with my dad, who was late for everything, it was true, but who had all the time in the world for love.

ROYAL IRISH ACADEMY

25 September 1773

Dear Sir,

In every letter of yours I am so enriched by useful information that I am put out of concert with all expression of gratitude because it cannot come up to the fullness of my heart. God granting me health, I shall soon have the pleasure of seeing you that you may read in some lineaments of my face what comes so faintly from this wretched quill.

I want to start writing like this. To resurrect this baroque language and infuse modern communication with some of its elegance. *Put out of concert by all expr of gratitude. #fullnessofheart #lineamentsofmyface #wretchedquill*

But it doesn't really work.

My friend Tasha is right: I miss these long handwritten letters — though who's got time to write them nowadays?

We're in the library of the Royal Irish Academy, another lovely space, this one with a vaulted ceiling and two levels of dark wooden bookcases running around the edges of the room. The academy was founded, a sign tells me, *as a society for promoting the study of science, polite literature, and antiquities.*

"I guess we won't find your books in here," my dad says, giggling quietly as we hang up our coats.

He explains to the librarians that we are here from Canada doing some ancestral research and looking for the correspondence of Charles O'Conor. Both women light up at the mention of the name.

"A most respected scholar," says one, immediately ascending a small ladder and pulling a volume from an upper shelf.

"A tireless crusader for Irish culture and civil rights," adds the other, carrying the volume to one of the long wooden tables for us and laying it out on a protective pillow, smiling at us as if we were heroes.

> *21 July 1762*
>
> *My Dear Sir,*
> *I do not love you more for the goodness of your heart and the talents of your mind than I esteem you for your political inflexibility.*

That first line is so good I whisper-read it aloud.

"Oh, why don't people write emails like that . . ." my dad muses. The librarian smiles. "Indeed."

> *The truth is, our people, broken by long habits of general distress, give up hope of relief. Fair weather once in sixty years was made for them, they came within cable's length of good anchoring, but a new storm arose; they put to sea again without rudder, without oars, without a compass. No wonder if, in a state of desperation, they should give themselves up for lost.*

I am agape at the lyricism of these letters, the composition as
well as the penmanship. They are small works of art, each one. I am
also impressed by the dedication and tenacity of the writer, Charles
O'Conor, whose research, the librarian informs us, helped to establish Ireland as the font of Gaelic culture and Irish culture as worthy
of honour, dignity, and preservation.

"In addition to his other political work, Charles O'Conor worked
tirelessly for the repeal of the Penal Laws," she tells us when she
returns with another small volume.

I thank her. Feel suddenly intrigued and energized.

"Now before you get too excited," my dad whispers, "Charles
O'Conor wasn't a relative of ours."

My shoulders crumple.

"But I'm looking for correspondence between O'Conor and
Thomas Egan, your great-great-great-great-grandfather." He turns,
gauges my response. "The one with the medical practice on O'Connell
Str—"

"I know, I know."

Satisfied, he begins flipping through his notes, looking for the
reference numbers he has written down, while I page through the
frangible documents.

Eventually we locate the letters, though my gr-gr-gr-gr-grandfather
Thomas Egan's writing isn't as rapturous or melodious as O'Conor's.
In fact, it's plodding, the letters simple petitions of support for Egan's
uncle to be named the local Catholic bishop. Still, my dad is thrilled
to have been able to read the original documents, and I am equally
thrilled that this branch of the family, at least, was in correspondence,
however mundanely, with an Irish hero.

Whatever that's worth.

There are a few more documents my dad would like to look up
on behalf of one of his genealogy buddies — he has several of these,
most of them women in their nineties who refer to him as *dear* — so

I tell him to take his time, that I'll amuse myself by reading more of O'Conor's eloquent letters.

Which I do, until I become interested in a woman on the opposite side of our large work table. She is about my age, slightly older, with dyed blonde hair and tailored clothing, tall leather boots and quietly expensive jewellery. Something in her poise and default facial expression reminds me of Mary Derry: reproof tinged with self-satisfaction. She isn't impolite to the library staff, but I notice that she makes no attempt to infuse any interaction with warmth.

Her research partner is in every way her foil: a mirthful, unassuming redhead with flyaway hair and flyaway laughter, who is as friendly as a golden retriever, immediately introducing herself to everyone she meets, enquiring after the new person's name, shaking hands enthusiastically with both hands, cupping the hand or elbow of her new acquaintance, saying something kind — *what a lovely name* or *what a pretty sweater* or *what a pleasure to meet you*. It might be nauseating if it weren't so genuine, but her expression is sincere, guileless, and each interaction feels as much like a blessing as a compliment.

The only way to know that the two women are sisters is to hear them introduce themselves as such, for not only are they dissimilar in demeanour, they also have entirely different accents: the uptight one speaks with a posh English accent, while the approachable one has a Dublin accent, as far as I can tell.

I keep catching the eye and smile of the Irish one, until eventually she comes around to our side of the table with an outstretched hand. Sarah — *lovely to meet you, and don't you both have such lovely brown eyes!* — is delighted to learn that my father and I are spending ten days in Dublin together. She hopes we are having a grand time, that our genealogical investigations are fruitful, that we have lovely weather, and that we manage to take in some of the town as well. If she can be of any help at all . . .

Sarah's older sister — *over there's Jane* — is motioning for Sarah to come back and look at the sheaf of papers she has been consulting for the last little while. Jane seems electrified by something, though in a muted way, her eyebrows doing all the work of expressing the emotion while the rest of her face remains slack, restrained. "This letter would suggest that our great-great-great-great-uncle Charles had dealings with a *Duke*," she tells Sarah, simultaneously emphasizing and lowering the volume of the word *Duke*.

Sarah reads the letter and squints a bit, Jane points to something and whispers a few pinched words, and Sarah laughs. A reaction that seems to annoy Jane, her eyeballs expressing her frustration by visiting the ceiling.

A few minutes later, Jane is convinced that she has found yet further evidence of their gr-gr-gr-gr-uncle Charles's connection to *Someone Very Important*, though she does not speak that final bit aloud. She mouths the words, stretching and overenunciating with her lips, her eyebrows at high mast. As Sarah peers over her sister's arm and reads the text in question, I notice Jane's posture, the frisson of pleasure this news has given her, the extra suggestion of dignity she now holds in her chin and her line of vision, which is now a few degrees higher than it was only moments ago.

For the rest of the morning, I watch the routine play out like a repetitive comedy: Jane discovering connections of her distant relatives to *VERY WEALTHY* people, the news being mouthed quietly enough to be considered restrained but loudly enough that everyone in the room can hear. Each discovery is accompanied by an expression of jaded satisfaction, a glance up into the ether, yet another confirmation of a superiority Jane seems to have always suspected. By contrast, the information seems to wash over Sarah like playful waves that splash into her face as she reads and smiles, shrugs like a child — *whatever* — and returns to what she was doing before.

It's impossible not to think about their dynamics of play as children. And not to wonder at why their accents are so different.

I whisper the discrepancy to my father, who listens for a minute and shrugs. But I'm too curious to let it go at that, so the next time Sarah stands up to collect some new material — she seems to be the workhorse of the duo; no shocking division of labour there — I follow her and ask.

"How is it that you and your sister have such different accents?" I ask, though it is none of my business. None.

Sarah laughs. She seems to preface every sentence with a few bubbles of laughter. "Oh . . . you've noticed that," she whispers, with a long round $\bar{o}$ and a light wisp of a t in noticed. "Well, you see, it's that my sister Jane lives in London."

Shamelessly, I pry further. "So, did you grow up in different places?"

Sarah shakes her head and laughs quietly. "No, we were both brought up here in Dublin and we did our studies together at Trinity College, but when Jane was about thirty-five, she got a job in London and she's been there ever since. Almost twenty years."

Regional accents often drain away from people after they move away, but this seems so extreme.

"But she sounds one hundred percent English!" I whisper. "There's no trace of Irish in her accent at all."

Sarah smiles, peers at me as if there is something she can't say. Her sister's accent might just be 100 percent put on, a song of superiority, but there could be something more painful there — a need to cut ties and reinvent herself? Whatever the case, I wish I hadn't asked.

"Yes, I suppose I'm used to it now," Sarah says, glancing over at Jane before turning back to me and winking. "But I could see as you might think we're from two different families entirely."

Sarah touches my arm before returning to her sister. It's a small gesture, simple and quick, but it's generous, for I feel the kindness in it. Nothing cloying or maudlin, just a smile conveyed by the hand. At the same moment, Jane looks up at me from the other side of the room and wince-smiles, an expression of faux politesse that empties me ever so slightly.

And this silent split-second interaction prompts the largest question I have about all of this.

Why does it *matter* the family we were born into, who and what those people were, whether they farmed or landlorded or fraternized with revolutionaries or corresponded with Very Important People or were solidly working class? Jane and I are caught in two sides of the same trap — snobbery and reverse snobbery — both of us scrambling to derive a measure of meaning and identity from the people who have come before us. It's natural to want to find out where we came from, fascinating and helpful to understand ourselves through our ancestry, certainly, but is it possible to care too much about family, to define ourselves too much by our predecessors and whatever they might have done, been, or owned? What do our antecedents actually mean to our present identity and how much of that should we claim?

Surely, it only *matters* who we are in the world right now, what we offer, share, give, inspire — today, tomorrow, and every day beyond that. Rather than defining ourselves by our personal histories, shouldn't we be looking to transcend them, to see the shadow they might cast on the ground and then move into our fullest light, the greatest potential of who we can become — how kind, how generous, how free — regardless of who came before us and whatever infamy or glory they might have attained?

Of course it's interesting to know what our great-great-great-great-grandfather did for a living (three guesses as to what gr-gr-gr-gr-grandmother did), but watching Jane ooze self-satisfaction with every Important connection reminds me of a comment of an ex-boyfriend, words that still, all these years later, make my heart heave.

We are where we're from, he said idly in reference to a dear friend of mine who hailed from an East Coast mining family and wasn't much of a reader. *It makes sense that she doesn't appreciate literature.*

I remember the floor cracking, a series of invisible fissures scribbling between us.

We are who we are, I replied. Or wish I'd replied. I believe I was too dumbfounded in the moment to say anything but *whaaaaat?*

∽

"Might I take a picture of you both for Twitter?" one of the librarians asks as my dad is returning materials and preparing to leave.

He looks utterly confused, as if he's just been addressed in Swahili and is expected to respond. "I-I-I beg your pardon?"

The woman shrugs sheepishly. "I'm sorry to trouble you. I just thought it would be grand to tweet out a picture of our patrons from Canada. You looked so lovely there at the table reading family papers with your daughter."

"You want to take our picture?" my dad confirms. "And send it to Twitter?"

"If it isn't any trouble."

My dad laughs. "No-no, none at all."

We sit back down at the table and strike a stilted posture of father and daughter consulting family papers merrily at the Royal Irish Academy. The librarian snaps the photo and says she'll tweet it out later this morning.

"I have no idea what that means," my dad admits as we put on our coats and leave the library. "And will it mean anything in three hundred years, I wonder?"

"Dad, it won't even mean anything three hundred minutes from now. That's the whole thing about Twitter."

My dad is quiet as he considers this, his face rumpling as we walk through the antechamber towards the main door. "But if it doesn't go on to mean anything, what's the point? It seems akin to jerking off."

The comment catches the attention of the security guard who signed us in a couple of hours ago. His head is still facing down, but his eyes are upon us when I turn to him and smile. He looks embarrassed to have been caught eavesdropping, straightens up quickly, clears his throat, and speaks deferentially, with something of a practiced guilt.

"I take a similar view on those matters, sir. Always have."

∽

We have a late lunch down the street at the cafeteria of the Kilkenny Design Centre's department store, which is a far more pleasant experience than it sounds. The food's excellent, for one thing — poached salmon, clam chowder, a couple of different quiches, grilled vegetables and potatoes, roasted chicken, roast beef, an array of salads, freshly baked bread, dozens of desserts — and the place is bright, uplifting, and bustling with students, elderly people, and every age in between.

We find a table by the window with a view over Trinity College and unload our plates from our trays.

"So, why do you care, Dad?" I ask, dividing up the quiche.

My dad looks up, confused. "Why do I care about what?"

I pause before rooting for specifics. Don't want to hurt his feelings.

"Well, why do you care about which parish your great-great-great-grandfather was born in and what he did for a living and who he wrote to? What does it give you to know that information? It just seems so irrelevant to me."

My dad chuckles. "Well, maybe you just need something more concrete. If we visit the spot where your great-great-great-great-grandfather had a medical practice two hundred and twenty-five years ago, something in your DNA might start to . . ." — he flutters one hand in the air — ". . . shimmer with a certain recognition."

He's joking. Though not entirely.

"Is that what happens to your DNA when you stand in front of buildings where your great-great-great-grandparents once lived?"

He laughs, though it's a forced laugh, more like a singing cough. "Well, I'm not sure I'd say that, but it does stir a certain curiosity . . ."

"Surely you're not looking for connections to Very Important People the way that woman in the Royal Academy seemed to be doing. She was so full of self-importance there was hardly room for it all on her face."

"Now, now," my dad admonishes.

Which reminds me of something I need to add: *The Way He Never Speaks Ill of People. Ever.*

"Okay, but didn't you find it nauseating the way she went on and on about her family's Important Connections?"

"Yes, I know what you mean . . . but her sister was good fun."

"Yes, I liked her too. But I kept wondering about what it is we are actually looking for when we do this. I mean, are people really entitled to some kind of dignity by association if their ancestors were great people? And what if they weren't? Do we just select those people out, or how does this work? It seems like some kind of ancestral cheat sheet to say *my grandfather was a hero and a genius, so I get all those marks too.* Meanwhile the other grandfather was a Nazi, but we're not going to talk about him. You know what I mean? And ultimately, how much does it *matter* who our forefathers and foremothers were? I mean, how much do they actually inform who we are today?"

My father's eyebrows are raised. Quite high. And he has stopped chewing. "Am I to try to answer all of those questions?"

I smile. "Yes."

He wipes his mouth. "Well, I agree that there's a certain amount of selective highlighting that sometimes goes on among certain genealogists, but I'm just interested in getting to know who people were, regardless of their circumstances." He pauses. "And I suppose we'll never know how much our ancestors inform who we are today, as you put it, but I guess I find it kind of fun to think about."

He lets his hand dance in the air in front of him. "It's all a kind of giant mystery. And the more I know, the more I want to know."

~

By the time we finish lunch, it's two o'clock. I begin stacking our plates and suggest we share a pot of tea and some dessert.

"But we should get going," my dad responds.

I stop stacking. "Oh, right, so . . . where . . . now?" I try to lift my voice, but shreds of dread weigh it down.

"The National Library," he says, as though it were obvious. "They're open until four thirty." He pulls out his notebook and begins flipping pages.

We haven't yet found a trace of what my dad has come looking for — those hypothetical documents that would give a definitive picture of the circumstances which might have led our people to emigrate — and I can feel him getting agitated, starting to worry that this entire trip will be a washout, that his efforts to locate the elusive clues and pieces will fail. He keeps furrowing his brow as he looks over his notes, flipping the pages brusquely.

It's terrible to watch him straining, to see his disappointment, to feel I might be letting him down. And it is not an unfamiliar sensation. Every one of my less-than-stellar years at university was accompanied by this same emotion, as well as my years of activism and aimless global wandering over the subsequent years. A feeling that I wasn't living up to my potential. No one ever said as much, but I often carried that suspicion, that I was somehow letting him down. That I might never do anything but continually let him down.

It passed eventually. Or I let it go, or he did. Or it was never there to begin with. Whatever the case, I'm suddenly anxious to get back to the library, to redouble my efforts, buck up, focus, find something, anything. Because there is something neither of us is saying, but of which we are both agonizingly aware: this is it. He won't be coming back here again. No one knows what the future will hold, but we do know one thing: this is my dad's last trip to Ireland. We either find what he is looking for this time or he leaves empty-handed. And I can't bear the thought of his going home disappointed.

"Okay, let's go," I say, bolting up from my seat and dusting crumbs from my hands.

"Oh!" he replies, hurrying to put his things in his briefcase. "I like your enthusiasm!"

NATIONAL LIBRARY

There are four systems of numbers per microfilm: one on the box itself (#P1219), one for the manuscripts (MS #253), one for the filing system (which begins, for reasons never explained, at 228; ergo 1 = 228), and then one for the pages themselves. What this means in practical terms is that #P1219: 1/315 is code for box 1219, manuscript 228, page 315. Except that many of the manuscripts are missing pages or begin on a page number other than one, and many aren't numbered at all. Meaning that there is no actual way to know you are on page 315. Even if you start at one and scroll through microfilm pages, one by one, counting until you reach 315. Which I've just done for the third time.

Already I want to gnaw my own leg off, but then it gets worse. After two full hours of confusion, bewilderment, pangs of self-doubt, and the manic rereading of the sign beside the microfilm machine — *TABHAIR FAOI DEARA GO BHFIUL FAIREACHAS A DHEANAMH TRI THEILIFS INMEANACH LE FISTAIFEAD LEANUNACH* — I am finally able to establish, conclusively, that there has been a series of secretarial errors when the material was transferred from hard copy onto microfilm, and there is, in fact, no reliable order to any of them, at all; they do not follow sequentially, and the numbers on the box, even when they have been correctly decoded, do not correspond exactly to the ones on the film, although some do.

Also, nearly everything on the films is illegible.

After deciding a full seven times not to throw my hands in the air and report all of this to my father — *I can figure this out I can figure this out I can figure this out* — I throw my hands in the air and report all of this to my father, who is sympathetic but doesn't believe me, I can tell. "Oh, don't worry about it. Just leave everything there, go for a walk, and I'll have a look," he says in a tone that is meant to be kind but feels patronizing. Not lost on me, in the midst of all of this, is the feeling that I have regressed, once again, though it's possible I have aged slightly. At the moment, I feel a full fifteen: slouchy, grumpy, and rebellious.

Donning my failure like a leaden suit two sizes too small, I walk, pound, down the stairs of the National Library and outside, where I notice a crowd, together with police cars and media cameras, gathered on the sidewalk outside the tall iron gates of Leinster House, the parliament of Ireland.

I approach a man with a large video camera on his shoulder and ask what's going on.

"They've formed a government at last," he says, his voice wholly devoid of excitement. "The new prime minister's about to come out."

"Where's the best place to stand?" shouts a rubicund woman with a strident voice.

"There's a spot over there," I say, indicating to a space by the gate.

The woman fiddles with her cell phone as she elbows unapologetically forward. "I help me to catch a snap of him as he drives past!" she calls, grabbing me by the arm and pulling me with her.

It's a small crowd, so we reach the front quickly. "Tell me when he drives past!" she instructs me, her eyes focused on her phone, finger at the ready. "Give me some warning, luv, a few secs to ready myself!"

I assure her that nothing is coming yet. No cars within view at all.

"No one's gonna believe I's standing right next to him as he drives past!" she says, pushing her crocheted wool hat back on her head, not taking her eyes off her phone, making a few adjustments to the camera settings, steadying her arm, straightening the view. "You tell me when to press the click!" she reminds me, and I assure her again.

"This one's just the police!" the cameraman calls out when the first car appears. The woman swats me on the arm, a playful gesture of excitement. She has her mouth open now, her tongue pressed to one side in concentration.

"You're telling me when to press the click!" she repeats, and I tell her to get ready, that there is another car on the way, moving slowly, drawing closer to the gate, almost here, wait, aaaaand . . . NOW.

The woman presses the click so forcefully she almost knocks the phone out of her own hands. I don't know if she noticed that the car had tinted windows, that even from this distance it was impossible to see anyone inside, but regardless, she's anxious to see the photo, lowering her head to the screen and pressing on it with thick fingers.

"Gobshite!" she calls, laughing with her entire body. "Look what I got!" She passes me her phone. It's a selfie, tongue and all. "Never mind," she says, taking her phone back and having another look. "They're all bleedin' eejets, anyway, aren't they? Politicians. Talkin' shite every time they open their gobs, bangin' on about what they're gonna do and bein' as useful as ashtrays on a motorbike. What do I want with a photo of that feckin' dosser on me mobile, anyway?"

She stuffs her phone into her coat pocket, adjusts her wool cap, and toddles away.

Already I feel better, but I decide to do a quick, brisk walk to clear my head. Less than a block away, on the corner of Nassau Street, a harpist is busking on the sidewalk. He appears tired, or sick of being a busker, possibly both, and his potential audience files past quickly, unengaged, except for a young man running his hand along a long metal gate as he walks, plucking the bars as if they were the strings of the harp. Around the corner is the entrance to the National Gallery. I can feel the right side of my body listing, aching to veer in and spend a few hours staring at art, but I manage to keep walking, which feels like such a commendable act of self-restraint that I decide to reward myself with a chocolate almond croissant at the bakery a few doors down.

The bakery's jammed, so it's ages before I'm able to make my order. The longer I wait, the deeper I delve into fantasies of halfway-between-heaven-and-reality pastry, silken marzipan cream, a drizzle of dark chocolate, slivers of toasted almond. The petite woman in front of me is taking forever to decide what she wants and I am just short of projectile salivating onto the back of her brown rain cloak when she orders a dozen mixed cakes in a nasally voice she must have been teased for in school.

They don't have almond croissants, so I order two plain ones and head back outside, where the woman in the brown coat is standing on the sidewalk waiting for a bus and mumbling about plum cake. I spend the remainder of the block inventing an elaborate story about where she is going and who the cakes are for, nearly convinced of the story's veracity by the time I finish spinning it out and wondering, as I often have, if this is a sign of creativity or neurosis. No conclusions.

At the end of the block, I meander towards the very green St. Stephen's Green, a city park with tall trees, parades of tulips, and clusters of people stretched out on the grass visibly ingesting the sunshine. I wish I could drag my dad out here, to lounge and chat and enjoy each other's company in this thin wedge of sunlight, to bask in the preciousness of this time together. But he doesn't seem able to see past his research to the magnificence of simply being together. Or maybe he does and I just wish he would notice it more. Either way, at the moment he is probably noticing my absence and wishing I would return to the research he wants and needs me to do.

As if I need to remind myself, *we're running out of time*.

The thought sends me skittering back to the National Library, where I find him sitting at the microfilm machines with his head in his hands. I touch his arm and he looks up, startled, before sighing loudly and collapsing forward, his body like a rumpled sock.

"None of these numbers make any *sense!*" he whimpers.

I try to focus on feelings of empathy rather than those of selfish vindication. "Oh, I know, Dad. I had the same trouble. Here, have a croissant . . ."

He sighs again, straightens himself, and reaches for the pastry looking grateful but withered.

We spend the next hour surreptitiously snacking on pastry while poring over the films together, rewinding and reviewing everything, slowly, from the beginning. We enlarge pages of faded, time-worn, hand-scrawled family trees, squint, decipher, double-check numbers, rewind and advance, count, enlarge and squint, check and recheck, until my dad finally reaches his breaking point, which he articulates with exasperated tones and the two quiet words "well, *fuck*."

I suggest calling it a day. Coming back tomorrow with fresh eyes.

He agrees. Touches my arm and thanks me for my dedication and endurance.

We box up the films and return them to the front desk, where my dad tries to explain the cataloguing problems to the staff, one of whom takes a few notes and nods sympathetically. "Our apologies to you, sir," she says. "How frustráting for you."

"It was more than frustráting," he replies, mimicking the accent. "An hour ago, I nearly screamed!"

The librarian's eyes widen as she laughs. "Oh dear. We don't often get screaming in the Reading Room. Well, thank goodness it didn't come to that."

"Well, it came close!" my dad says, inhaling loudly and then giggling. "It was my daughter who saved me! She's a tremendous help," he says, clutching my arm.

The librarian rests her hands on the desk and smiles. "Aren't you lucky to have each other."

Words that corral a thousand tears into a hard knot in the middle of my throat.

~

Only when we are outside do I remember to tell my dad about the new government being formed and how I happened upon the new prime minister as he was driving away. I am partway into the story of the woman who tried to take the picture, when my dad cuts me off. "So, who's the new prime minister?"

"Oh . . . uh . . ." I was so intent on my exchange with the woman and her camera that I never bothered to get the name.

"Well, which party was he from, Fine Gael or Fianna Fáil?"

I could tell him the colour and texture of the wool used to crochet the hat of the woman taking the picture, the string of technicolour expressions she used. But he isn't interested in any of that.

"I . . . uh . . . heard his name was Feckin' Dosser."

My dad looks confused. Squints. "I don't know him. He must be from one of the smaller parties."

THE LIFFEY

We've decided to walk home via O'Connell Street, to see if we can find number thirteen, the building where my gr-gr-gr-gr-gr-grandfather had a medical practice 225 years ago, when O'Connell was called Sackville Street.

"Hey, let's cross at the Ha'penny Bridge," my dad suggests, explaining that the name of the narrow pedestrian wooden bridge dates back to a time when there was a charge of a halfpenny to use it. There is no official charge now, though the heart commands an offering to the guys sitting on both sides of the narrow arc with cans in hand.

One man, a middle-aged fellow in workboots and a thin wool coat, looks as though he must have sat through a downpour, his green-black coat drenched tight to his body. His beard is the grey of ashes. He wears every posture of resignation, looks down, away, at his hands, and mumbles shame-soaked *tanks* or *ga'bless* when coins are dropped into his cup. Beside him is a stack of books wrapped in a clear plastic bag. They're thin volumes, possibly poetry, but I can't make out any of the titles.

At the end of the bridge is a collection table for the Irish Soup Kitchens.

"Unemployment's over fourteen percent," one of the people manning the table tells me. "Jobs is rare as hen's teeth. Least we can do is give the lads a bit o' stew, isn't it?"

I turn to look at my dad but he's not beside me. He's gone on ahead, is folding into a crowd of people on the other side of the road. I watch him turning his head, looking for me.

"I'll come back tomorrow," I tell the man, who nods wearily. "I will," I insist, but the man's eyes have already moved on to a woman who has stopped at the table and is reaching for her wallet. I mumble apologies and step away.

Run to catch up with my dad, who hasn't noticed any of this at all.

"I've been thinking about your earlier question," my dad muses, "about why I care so much about all of this. And I wonder if being a genealogist might be a bit like being a birder. It strikes me as being somewhat similar."

Which is something I have wondered myself.

You see, my partner is a birder. Which doesn't mean that he enjoys watching and admiring birds. No-no. That's only part of it. The *being a birder* that my dad is referring to is the part that involves waking up in the middle of the night to a *ping!* which indicates that a rare bird has been spotted somewhere in the province, getting up, and driving for, let's say, up to five hours to stand by the side of a sewage lagoon with binoculars pinned to the eyes, monitoring, for hours, in the rain, hundreds of gulls, all of which are dull grey and white, in search of one with a slightly darker grey patch on the back of the head — nearly identical, yes, but a different *species* — finally seeing it, driving five more hours back home, and calling it a great day. A rare sighting. Not necessarily the first time seeing this particular bird, but the first time seeing it *there*.

I am not making any of that up.

And, indeed, I have found myself thinking of sewage lagoons and the staring out at hundreds of dull grey and white gulls in search of one with a slightly darker grey patch on the back of the head when I am scrolling through pages and pages of illegible eighteenth century parish records in search of a birth record with the name Faunt on it.

"So what *is* that?" I ask. "What is it, do you think, that fascinates you guys about that level of minutiae when it's so meaningless to someone on the outside? And why is it all about the proof, the documentation? Why isn't the possibility or the larger story enough?"

My dad tosses his head back, looks up, as if the answer might be hovering above him, dangling from a balloon. "Well," he says, stopping for a moment. He breathes deeply, his chest visibly rising. He sends his right hand out in front of him, as if he is about to declare a grand proclamation. "I don't know." There is a degree of finality in his voice, a sort of *and that's that* intonation that makes it sound like the final word on the subject, until he adds, "Maybe it's like opera for Michael . . ."

∽

A bit of background: my fairy stepmother Michael has been enamoured of opera since the moment he heard his first tremulous aria as a university student. He became a devoted opera fan, devouring the repertoire as if it contained the elixir of life, travelling vast distances to hear so-and-so sing such-and-such (still does), planning every holiday around opera seasons in foreign cities (still does), and letting not a day go by wherein opera is not enjoyed in some fashion. For years, Michael drove a truck for the post office because the pay was good, the overtime was better, and the job allowed him to plan his vacations around opera schedules.

The first time I invited a friend to spend the weekend with me at my father and Michael's house, I was in university. It was the 1980s. My friend had never been in a gay couple's house before. Such things (gay couples' houses) hardly existed back then. There was a Greco-Roman statue of wrestling men on the dining room table, feather boas draped over the hallway mirror, a *Playgirl* calendar in the bathroom, and endless giggly antics as my dad and Michael teased each other over meals, but after a full weekend, the only question my friend asked was *Why do they listen to so much opera?*

Well, I said, relieved but trying to be casual. *I don't really know.* There might have been a degree of finality in my voice, a sort of *and that's that* intonation that made it sound like the final word on the subject, because, as I recall, we went on to talk about something else.

Three decades later, I am still without a satisfactory explanation for the correlation of gay men and opera, but this is not what my father is referring to when he suggests that being a birder or being a genealogist might be *a bit like opera for Michael*. What he means, I believe, is Michael's encyclopedic knowledge of the subject, so vast and specialized it spins the eyeballs of anyone who doesn't share his interest.

"Whatever it is, the point is to care a great deal about *something*," my dad says with a professorial tone of conclusion. "Because what would life be without a passionate devotion to something? Actually, I'll tell you exactly what it would be: Very Boring. And probably quite depressing."

When we reach O'Connell Street, a rail-thin man holds a cardboard sign that says, *Don't Be Doomed*, the second O having been added at a later date, squeezed in beside the first O with a slightly different pen. He is speaking softly, preaching, perhaps, although no one on the sidewalk is paying any attention. "Jesus died for your salvation,"

he says weakly as we pass, adding the afterthought, "It was like . . .
a free gift."

Across the wide boulevard is the GPO, the General Post
Office, a grand Georgian building with six imposing columns
at the entranceway. As I read on our first day here, this building
became the headquarters of the Easter Rising and it was almost
completely destroyed in the fighting. In honour of the centenary,
there is a large exhibit about the revolt and a line of tourists gathered outside.

"Shall we go and see that?" I ask, curious to learn more.

My dad glances across the street and takes a deep breath. "Well . . .
maybe not today . . . or . . . if you want to . . ." He turns back to face the
buildings on our side of the street and squints for the numbers. "Oh,
look, there's number seven . . . we're getting close to number thirteen
. . . it should be in the next block . . ."

I take a last glance at the GPO, knowing full well we'd be scouring the building had the cousin of a great-great-uncle twice-removed
once trimmed the toenails of someone who had been involved in
the uprising. And I can't help thinking, yet again, how much more
interesting all of this would be if there were some valorous elements
to grasp, some intrepid Irish rebel or civil rights crusader, some
long-suffering suffragette. A story. If we were delving into an unacknowledged history of some kind, perhaps, looking to give voice to
a forgotten people.

But we're headed to a doctor's office. The workplace of a member
of the Royal Society who once wrote a letter to an Irish hero. Surely
it's understandable if that does not stir the depths of my soul. In
some ways, it's probably a good thing my ancestors weren't magnificent heroes. I have a feeling I might have clung to such a story like
a flag, used it as a badge of identity, self-righteousness — not unlike
the pretentious woman I spent half the morning dissing in the Royal
Academy, now that I think of it.

But it's not just the lack of valorous characters or a stirring familial plot line. I am also less than ravenous for my own history because I have never had to hunger for it. On the contrary: like most other Canadian children, I was force-fed Anglo culture, its mores and institutions, its colonial narratives taught to us as history, presented proudly and unquestioningly as fact. By the time I finished school, I felt bloated by it all, weary of its dominance and implied superiority, ashamed at the arrogance, the smugness, the blind conceit. What I longed for were the stories that had no such prominence, the buried histories, the quieter voices. The things that never got written down, that left no record. I wanted to winkle out the information where I could and imagine the rest. Create what was believably true but unprovable.

But this isn't the time for such imaginings. We're on a birding expedition. Standing, in the rain, looking out over an expanse of grey stone buildings and keeping our eye out for one with the number thirteen on its front.

The GPO shrinks behind us as we continue up the street, passing number eleven — "We're getting close!" my dad calls excitedly — and then number . . . fifteen. Meaning that the building in the middle, the former home and medical practice of Dr. Thomas Egan, graduate of Montpellier University, member of the Royal Irish Academy and our most distinguished relative, is now the temporary home of Hugh Grant and Meryl Streep. A movie theatre called the Savoy, currently playing *Florence Foster Jenkins*.

My dad and I stand on the sidewalk with our heads tilted back, staring up at the giant poster.

"Well," my dad says, disappointed, perhaps, but being a sport about it, "there *is* a certain family connection . . ."

Which is true, in that I grew up with Florence Foster Jenkins. Not the person but the legend, her famous recording, her unforgettable voice. A wealthy New York City socialite, the real-life Jenkins loved music, fraternized with famous musicians, and dreamed of being an opera singer. Unfortunately (for her), she wasn't just a terrible

singer, she was outrageously bad, unable to sing remotely in tune
and with a taste for garish costumes and histrionics that made her
concerts madly entertaining — though not in the way she intended.
Rumour had it Cole Porter used to have to bang his walking cane
on the floor while listening to keep himself from exploding with
laughter. Because of her money and connections, Jenkins managed
to book herself a recital at Carnegie Hall (sold out weeks in advance,
thousands turned away at the door) and then she issued a recording,
which my parents used to play from time to time.

It was the combination of abysmal singing and oblivious sincerity that made it so terribly, painfully, funny. Sometimes my mother, a
person of bountiful compassion, would try to point out some of the
less disastrous bits, even chide us for laughing, but trying to suppress
her own laughter eventually made it leak out all the harder, so no
matter how often we listened to it, that Florence Foster Jenkins
recording reduced our entire family to hysterics every time.

I ask my dad if he remembers the way my younger brother used
to like to stand on a kitchen chair wearing a tea cozy on his head,
singing Florence Foster Jenkins's rendition of Mozart's Queen of
the Night aria with extra-wobbly vibrato, deliberately not hitting
any of the top notes.

"Who could forget that? That was one of the highlights of the
1970s," my dad replies casually, looking at his watch. "Shall we go in
and see it? It only started about . . . ten minutes ago."

And we do. In an odd pairing of family circumstances, my father
and I buy tickets to watch Meryl Streep play Florence Foster Jenkins
at the hallowed address where my father's mother's father's mother's
mother's father had a medical practice 225 years ago. I have no idea if
this is a significant genealogical moment or just a pleasantly absurd
one. Either way, the film's pretty bad, pat and two-dimensional, but
revisiting the story under such preposterous circumstances makes
for great fun.

~

On our way out, we get turned around and aren't sure which direction to head, when we notice a small pub tucked into one side of the theatre. It looks traditional, typical, inviting.

"Why don't we go in and have a pint before we head home?" my dad suggests.

As we get closer, a small sign above the doorway pulls into focus and knocks us both to a standstill.

13.

"*WUUUUUH!* Oh my *goodness!*" His voice manages to rise a full octave over the course of those few words. "Here it is! Number thirteen!"

We push through the door.

The pub is dim, comfortable, with dark woodwork, a long bar, low ceilings, and dozens of round tables full of people curled around drinks. Nothing about it suggests it was once a medical practice, but the building itself, the basic structure of it, could certainly be original. We walk to the back of the pub in search of a quiet place to sit, but a man has just fallen down a flight of stairs in what seems to have been an alcohol-induced tumble and there is a flurry of activity around him. There is one small table available beside the pub's live entertainment, but the singer is something of an Irish folk equivalent of Florence Foster Jenkins, so after my dad takes a good look around and stops to admire a few thick ceiling beams, he suggests we go somewhere else instead.

"How about that place that John recommended in Smithfield? The pub right near our flat?"

We cross the cobbled lanes of O'Connell Street and begin to wend our way through the back streets towards Smithfield.

"So, did any strands of your DNA start dancing around in there?" I ask.

My dad flutters his hands quickly in front of his face. It's a hallmark gesture and can convey great excitement, lukewarm appreciation, or abject revulsion. "Well . . . not exactly," he admits. "But research is like that. You always end up having to travel to a number of dead ends before stumbling upon something interesting, so I just try to stay curious and keep an open mind."

"Yes, I've been trying to do that too, but one of the things I've found myself wondering is what if we inherit something, way down the line, that was acquired by questionable means?"

"What do you mean, like stolen property?"

"Yeah, and maybe it was stolen generations earlier, and maybe the person didn't even realize it was stolen when they acquired it. Do we inherit the perks, talents, and property of our ancestors, or also their sins?"

There is a long pause. "I'm not sure what sins you're referring to."

"Well, no, nothing specific. I'm just speaking in general terms. I mean, this whole ancestry business is really about identity, isn't it? Not just who the people were who came before us, but who that makes us. And it's terrific when it offers clarity and strength, or maybe a sense of union, but what if it doesn't? Are we *required* to find our identity among the people who came before us?"

My dad is quiet. He is walking swiftly, purposefully, with his eyes on the sidewalk. "There's no requirement," he says in such a deflated tone that I want to shove my words back into my mouth, rewind time, and start again.

It never occurred to me before now that my rejection of my British heritage, this lineage, this ancestry, might have felt to my dad like a rejection of him. All those years I spent trying to win his approval, was I actually the one withholding my approval of him, his family and roots, our shared heritage?

"Sorry, Dad. I'm not criticizing, really. I'm just trying to understand. And it's quite complex, isn't it? Our histories are rich and interesting, of course, but maybe they're just a starting point."

"A starting point for what?"

"Well, identity, I guess. Because some identities can give us a sense of who we are, but they can also limit us, keep us from seeing the potential of who we might be *beyond* how we have always defined ourselves, don't you think? Isn't it equally liberating sometimes to transcend our stories, not understand ourselves solely by our biographies but become the authors of our own lives?"

My dad walks a few steps in silence. "That sounds like something a writer would say."

"Ha, maybe, but I find myself wondering if this focus on biological ancestry and DNA and so on is one aspect of a larger quest. Maybe it's more multidimensional than that, as much a longing for self-awareness and wholeness as a need to know what so-and-so's birth certificate looked like."

Another pause.

"Huh."

I wait for him to say more, but he doesn't.

"And how does the concept of reincarnation fit into all of this? I mean, how do you trace past lives of the soul? I doubt that it neatly follows family bloodlines, so what about that kind of inheritance?"

My dad walks on without a word. In his mind, I have asked a question as cogent and germane as *But what about the property rights of leprechauns, Dad? Have you considered that?* So I am about to say a bit more but he speaks first, deftly changing the subject.

"I'm not sure I've mentioned that Thomas Egan's research mostly dealt with urine," he says.

I stop. Turn to see if he's serious. He is.

I abandon all thoughts of reincarnation and face the facts at hand.

"Our most distinguished ancestor dealt in piss," I confirm.

He nods deeply, enjoying himself, but deadpan. "Aren't you proud to be descended from a urine specialist?"

∽

When we reach Capel Street, a thoroughfare in a trendy neighbourhood lined with small shops and cafés, two young men pass us on
the sidewalk. One is in the midst of telling a story and his friend is
almost doubled over with laughter. "Well, that takes the biscuit!"
the friend says, stepping around us onto the road. The storyteller
ploughs rudely between us, knocking my dad on the shoulder without apology. My dad is fine, but I curl into his arm protectively. It's
his left arm, the one with the tremor, and when I nestle into it I am
shocked at the strength of its jolting, as if it were a powerful electri-
cal cable, pulsing and jerking.

"You'd better let go," he says, yanking his arm away. The gesture
startles me. My dad's a cuddler, always has been. Long, amorous
embraces and snuggles are his signature. He's never pulled away
from me like that before, ever. I can't believe how heartbroken it
makes me feel.

We walk the rest of the way to the pub with a chasm of space
between us, a cruel electricity holding us apart.

∽

Delaney's looks like a biker hangout from the outside, but we go
in anyway and it is full, beyond full. Whatever the legal capacity of
the pub is, there are twice as many people inside. It is impossible to
tell what the place itself looks like because there are people along
every wall and scrunched into every corner. Somehow, though, it
does not feel overly crowded or claustrophobic; it feels welcoming,
alive. There are no televisions. Not one. There is no wifi. People are
engaged only with each other. It's revolutionarily pleasant.

The customers are of all ages. And all types, whatever that means:
students, couples, groups of fashionable women, groups of unfash-
ionable women, rough-looking men in leather vests, hipster men

with trendy eyewear that makes them look insectile, young people with instruments, old men with tweed caps on their heads and holes in the sleeves of their sweaters, and everyone with beer. Everyone. Including, after a bit of manoeuvring, my father and me. As we are carrying our pints away from the bar, a young woman gets up and sits on a friend's lap to allow my dad and me to sit down, so we call out our thanks and share a dark-red velvet seat along the wall.

The Guinness is exceptional: so creamy, frothy, bitter, and rich, it is as close to a fine cappuccino as beer can get. I take a long, chewy sip and groan loudly; my dad does the same. The men at the table beside us are talking politics, how it's all gone to shite, how they're all plonkers and arse weeds, acting the maggot, and that bloody American! "You can tell that one was weaned on the hind tit," yells one man to the nodding assent of his friends. "'The wheel's turning but the hamster's dead," calls another man, and the entire table agrees.

I can barely jot the phrases down fast enough, my pen scratching words onto the cardboard coaster around my sweating glass, when some live music starts up at the other end of the pub and drowns out all voices.

The music becomes boisterous and acoustic, at the low end of genius but brilliant in spirit and tone. It is joy by fiddle, laughter by accordion, Ireland through to the bone.

At one point, my dad leans over and shouts into my ear. "Getting back to our earlier conversation . . . I keep thinking that it's only because of his obsessive devotion to all the various details and minutiae that Michael gets so much out of every opera he attends!" he calls.

It is an absurd conversation to be having right now, right here, but I shout back into his ear anyway.

"Yes! And likewise with how much Jay sees when he looks out at a shoreline filled with birds! He sees how they all fit into larger patterns of migration routes and breeding ranges and so on, and the rest of us just see dots!"

My dad sends his head bobbing way up and down to let me know he's heard and agrees.

He's been out on a couple of birding expeditions with Jay — well, one — and came home bewildered by the experience. "Well, we did a lot of standing around and looking up through binoculars, and there were some birds," my dad reported with an effort at enthusiasm, "but they all seemed to be brown." He paused, looking for something positive to say. Because that is what he does. Eventually, he added, "At times there were some lovely cloud formations . . ."

My dad turns and shouts, "And for both of them, their obsessions are quasi-religious experiences!"

I give him an exaggerated nod.

He leans in again, cups my ear. "It's quite paradoxical!"

I turn and shrug. Mouth the word *why?*

He cups my ear again. "Because it's those very small and seemingly mundane details which allow them to connect to something so vast and tra—sen—t!"

"So WHAT?" I shout.

"SO VAST AND TRA—SE—T!" He is shouting into my ear but I still can't make it out.

I shrug and point to the music, my dad nods, and we return to our Guinness, wait for the next lull. At which point my dad sighs with relief. "I was saying it may look like they're just obsessed with small, irrelevant details — and some of the time that's all it is — but that's what also allows them to connect to something so vast and *transcendent*."

"Oh, *transcendent!* Yes, so is that what genealogy allows you to experience? Is that what's on the other side of all of these details for you, a kind of transcendence?"

He looks pensive, takes a long sip of beer. Inhales, looks up, to the ceiling, beyond. "Well, maybe in a way," he says at last, "but it's more like the feeling of staying up late at a cottage long after everyone else has called it a night and seeing a partly finished thousand-piece puzzle on the table. I could just say, *Oh forget it, who cares*, and go to bed. But for some reason I've decided that I want to stay up and see how it all fits together, and right now I'm zeroing in on all the bits of sky, all those very, very similar bits of blue, and the frustrating part is that a lot of them are missing, as you well know, but when I find a piece that actually fits together, WUUUUUH!" — he whoops so loudly that people at neighbouring tables glance over — "It's so *satisfying!"*

"That sounds more like an orgasm than transcendence, Dad," I say, smiling at the people around us.

"Well, those two things are quite connected!" He throws his hands up playfully, then considers. "But I think it's more like a jigsaw."

He's told me a version of this analogy before: that all of these documents and family trees and clues about who might have been connected to whom — it's all one big scavenger hunt, an endless series of mysteries to be solved and understood, a four-dimensional puzzle that goes on for centuries.

"And who doesn't love a puzzle?!" he asks.

When my brothers and I were kids, our grandparents would sometimes give us *brain-teasers* for Christmas: interlocking rings, spirals and twists of metal that had to be stacked, turned, threaded, and pulled in just the right way, and in just the right order, to be successfully pulled apart. When my older brother unwrapped his, he would stop everything and sit in the large flowered armchair in the living room until he solved it, even if it took the rest of the morning and there were still presents left to unwrap. I tended to unwrap mine and say *Oh a puz-zle* with strained gratitude, before nudging it under the sofa and reaching for another gift.

"I've never been big on puzzles," I remind him.

"Or maybe your puzzles are stories!" he calls as the music picks up again. "And the writing is" — he shimmers his hands in a long arc in front of him, as if he were miming a bird lifting into flight — "your way of puzzling life out!"

We lift our glasses and swill the last of the Guinness.

~

On the way back to John's, we are both quiet, enjoying the quiet, and I am sifting through the day, our conversations.

"It's all about focus, isn't it?" I ask as we reach the cobblestone alleys of the distillery.

My dad is watching his feet as we walk, hunched slightly. He walks this way more and more. "What's all about focus?"

"All of these obsessions, or puzzles, or whatever they are: your genealogy, Michael's opera, Jay's birding, my writing — they're all about focus. It's almost arbitrary what the point of focus is, because it's really all about what opens when we devote ourselves to some-thing, when we focus on something, really *focus*."

"Being in the zone," my dad says. "That's what one of my piano buddies calls it when she's practising and really getting into a piece and — *floop!* — three hours go by."

"Well, yes, and what preceded that moment was probably a lot of tedious practising."

We've reached the door to John's building. I motion for my dad to go ahead.

"I'm not sure I follow you," he says, staying where he is.

"You don't have to follow me, Dad. Go ahead. I'll hold the door."

"No-no, I'm not sure I'm following what you're *saying*. And I'll hold the door. *You* go ahead."

After an awkward two-step, we both make it inside and wait for the elevator. It arrives carrying two young women, university students, I'd guess. They smile and glide past us, leave tailings of perfume.

"I mean that when your friend practises, it's not just that she loses track of time," I continue, "because we can all lose track of time getting distracted or sucked into the internet or whatever, and it's not the same feeling. At all. That's draining and disorienting, almost depressing. But losing track of time with deep intentional focus is the opposite: it's hard work, but it's energizing."

"Yes, we often come out with more energy than we went in with," my dad says.

"Exactly, so what *is* that? What are we tapping into when we are so deliberately focused like that? It's so powerful."

My dad considers, staring up into one corner of the elevator until it arrives on John's floor. "I think it's just the product of going really deeply into one thing instead of flitting around on the surface of a lot of different things," he says as we walk down the hallway. "You never really get anywhere if you just stay on the surface."

"Like relationships . . ."

"Yes, I guess it is." He stands in front of John's door and waits for me to unlock it. Keys are tricky at the best of times.

"So, maybe focus is a kind of devotion, a kind of love." I unlock the door. Motion for my dad to go ahead.

He smiles, looks satisfied, almost serene. "Yes, I think it is a kind of devotion." He walks into the kitchen and sets his soft leather brief-case on the table, removes his cap, his coat, sits down at the table, and opens his computer. "Or it's an obsessive quirk!" he declares, opening his email. "But quirks are wonderful things! Frankly, I feel sorry for people who *don't* have obsessive quirks!" He looks up, mystified. "What on earth do they do on their holidays?"

∽

After dinner and the news, I retreat to my bedroom, unlatch the window, and push it open a few inches to let something of the night in. And there is something about the temperature, or the smell of the cold, perhaps, or the sight of a small crescent of the moon in a blue-black sky, that makes a scene spill out of memory.

It was the summer my son turned four. We were living in a cabin in the woods on the Bruce Peninsula while Jay, an ecologist, was doing work in the area. There was no electricity or running water, no city or town or neighbour for miles, just a network of wildlife and a depth of quiet that surrounded and moved into us all. The nights were hollow, empty of traffic, noise, but sewn with living silence, the stillness that allows quiet life to sing. One evening, after our son had fallen asleep between us on our large shared bed, Jay and I were whispering, enjoying a rare uninterrupted conversation until he said *shhht!* and held up one finger.

He'd heard something. A bear, perhaps. They lived all around us. Or maybe a rattlesnake. They lived under the cabin.

What is it? I whispered.

That ovenbird just had a nightmare, Jay said casually, lowering his hand.

What? I laughed. *How do you know it had a nightmare? How do you even know what kind of bird it is?*

He spoke matter-of-factly, as though imparting common knowledge. *It was definitely an ovenbird, and they don't sing at night.*

I laughed again. I was used to teasing him about birding: the hours (and hours and hours) spent staring through binoculars at small distant dots, the compiling of coded lists of birds seen in various places, the crazed expeditions to remote areas in search of rare birds that had been spotted out of range, the crestfallen explanations that the rare bird in question had flown away (surprise!) before he'd arrived. There was a lot to make fun of.

How do you know birds even dream?

Why wouldn't they? His voice sounded punctured. *Anyway, it's the only thing that explains why it just sang like that, in the dark, and so briefly.*

I paused, listened, heard nothing.

Jay returned to our conversation, whispering about something I no longer remember. What I do remember is my sudden awareness of how much he heard that I did not, how attuned he was to beings I did not even register, to lives and dreams I had no awareness of, no connection to at all.

Later, as we tilted on the cusp of sleep, he whispered, *Can you hear that distant peeping?*

I couldn't. *Is it the ovenbird again?*

No, listen: they're migrating songbirds. They avoid predators by travelling at night.

I lifted my head from the pillow. Still didn't hear them.

Some biologists believe they use the stars to navigate, he whispered. *That peeping is their way of staying connected to each other.*

Our son moaned and turned in his sleep, tucked a foot under the small of my back. I lay for a while, listening to Jay descend into sleep, listening to the night quilt of cicadas, the faint descant of coyotes yipping in the distance.

And then I heard them.

Pinpricks of light in the darkness. Wisps of song falling from the night sky. A matrix of astral passage, of miraculous flight. An ancestral map spun into wings.

A casual, unassuming portal to infinity.

THURSDAY

10 BOW STREET

I wake up in the wee hours unable to sleep. And, as I do from time to time when my mind needs quieting, I calm myself by thinking about frogs.

Growing up on the edge of wild fields and forests, some of my fondest childhood memories are of lying stock-still at the edge of a large pond watching kingfishers and herons, water snakes and muskrats. I was also a great admirer of frogs. I loved the way they floated for ages, immobile, monitoring their world, hunting with their tongues, diving and crossing the pond doing the very whip kick I used to do lengths with a Styrofoam flutter board at swim practice at the YMCA. Frogs delighted me, relaxed me, made me quiet, alert, peacefully alive.

Years later, in grade ten biology class, our teacher presented us with a terrarium full of frogs. The animals jumped and tried to climb the walls of the enclosure, their soft white bellies pressing against the glass — reaching, stretching, reaching — until they toppled over and on top of each other, to the delight of the class. Then, without warning, the teacher dropped a rag soaked with chloroform into the terrarium and sealed the top with a heavy black lid.

Gradually, the animals slowed their jumping and climbing, the boys in the class snickered, the girls moaned and gasped. And after a few minutes of silent screaming, all the frogs were dead. The teacher pulled them out one by one, the lifeless bodies dangling from his hand like uncoiled springs. Each frog was laid on a wooden board and fastened, belly up, with long pins. We were instructed to take the scalpels we had been given, make slits in the stomachs, and peel back the skin. Which I might have done had I not left the classroom and stormed off the school grounds rigid with fury. I wandered through rambling fields kicking stones, smearing tears and snot, yanking tall grasses until they sliced my hands, collapsing into the wholesome smell of mud and watching a slow scenery of clouds that eventually put me to sleep.

A few days after the frog massacre, the biology teacher saw me in the hallway and asked me to explain my sudden departure from his class, my continued absence. He was concerned, he told me with a concerned expression and in concerned tones, about what he called my *oversensitivity*. Death is a natural part of life, he explained. Which lead me to ask whether or not it would be natural, therefore, to follow him home and chloroform his dog. *Dogs are not frogs*, he countered. *Amphibians don't feel death as acutely.*

The substance of the rest of the conversation did not make it into the scrapbook of my memory, but I do remember his making the point that without the frog assignment, which would make up a significant portion of the final mark, I might be in danger of failing the class. And I must have told him that danger of failure was my favourite form of risk, because I didn't attend another biology class until the naturally-chloroformed-to-death frogs had all been labelled, lacquered, and mounted around the classroom like disemboweled taxidermic trophies.

The following semester, I ran into similar trouble in English class. Books that had once been my love, my lifeline, my passion and passage to the sublime were one day chloroformed and laid out on planks of wood: our desks. Employing a logic and detachment frightening to me even now, we were instructed to slit open the soft bellies of these stories and extract their innards one by one: plot, theme, evidence of character development, evidence of narrative structure, evidence of foreshadowing. I didn't march out of that class in protest; I don't remember even being aware of the similarity of the dissection. The only thing I knew was that by the end of that semester, reading had ceased to be a source of pleasure or inspiration.

For years afterwards, I read nothing but textbooks and newspapers, both of which I consumed like a ravenous fire, fuelling and confirming the despair I felt about the world. I became swollen with information, began mistaking knowledge for wisdom, facts for truth, cleverness for acumen, and I walked the world with an emptiness that was, at times, almost too great to bear.

Stories of the imagination were not only dead to me, they seemed frivolous, pointless, incapable of solving any of the earth's problems, which were colossal and impending. Only after I left university and began to travel did I rediscover the solace of story. The tantalizing pleasure of language. Words as vessels of joy, and of power.

By the time I landed in Czechoslovakia, I was ripe for the miracle of a dissident playwright becoming president of his country, a writer being seen as the guardian of the soul of the nation. I traded books with Tasha and other expats, English-language novels and poetry suddenly a currency of the highest value. In one of many English classes I conducted around the city, I chose an excerpt of *Animal Farm* to study with the group. *Has anyone read it?* I asked the first day. A few arms went up. One man see-sawed his hand. *I typed some parts*, he said. *For samizdat*. The secret copying and circulation of books that had been banned by the communist regime. If you were one of those willing to risk imprisonment for the sake of literature, he explained, you would one day receive a book and a copy-in-progress, stop your life for twenty-four hours, type like mad, all night, if necessary, and then pass the job on to the next trusted person, who would pick it up from where you had left off, and do the same. This way, copies of banned books were continually created and distributed under decades of communist oppression.

I was gobsmacked when I heard this. Not because I was learning about it for the first time, but because of how casual the man was in his description of the task, and the tired nodding and shrugging of many others in the class, as though, yeah, haven't we all stayed up typing Orwell and Huxley until dawn.

Well, I hadn't. (Still haven't.) But stories changed for me that day. They came back to life. Unpinned themselves from the dissection table and resumed their place in the pond, where they have reasserted their majesty, their importance, and where they have swum, observed the world, made me quiet, alert, peacefully alive, ever since.

~⌒

THE LIFFEY

On our morning walk along the river, my dad points out flags for the Dublin Gay Theatre Festival. It's on all this week. The festival's patron saint is Oscar Wilde, the great Irish writer and playwright convicted of "gross indecency" and sentenced to two years of imprisonment with hard labour for his suspected relationships with men.

"I used to meditate on a line from Wilde's last work, *De Profundis*, when I was coming out," my dad tells me, staring into the distance. *"It is only by realising what I am that I have found comfort of any kind."*

I leave a parcel of silence around the sentence. It's been so long since I've heard him say anything like that, and it reminds me of how he used to walk in the world, full of questions, agonies, admonitions, fears that he was making the greatest mistake of his life, leaving a woman and children he loved to pursue a life that was still such a mystery to him, still so clandestine and condemned. He found comfort in literature, I remember him telling me, and in music, and in the company of men who had been brave enough to stand up and declare themselves. Men proud to be gay.

We make a small detour to stop by the festival box office and enquire about the shows, eventually settling on *Erect but Unstable*, a one-man show by a fellow Canadian. My dad is also interested in a couple of other shows, one called *F*CKING MEN*, with a poster which depicts a coterie of buff men lounging all over each other in various stages of flexing and undress.

"Why don't you do that one on your own, Dad?" I suggest, catching the eye of the box office woman and winking.

"Yes, that one might not be your kind of thing," my dad says, consulting the programme. "Oh, look, there's a matinée on Sunday. I could go then."

"Instead of church," I tease him.

He laughs, then gasps. "Oh, now that reminds me of the time I wanted to do an erotic massage course with Michael!"

I watch the box office woman lean forward, casually tilting an ear towards the conversation.

"I had just joined that Mennonite choir I used to sing with, so we ended up not being able to do the massage course."

I squint. "Why? You mean people in the choir would have disapproved? How would they even have known?"

"Oh, no, it was nothing like that. It was that the erotic massage course ran over the whole weekend and apparently it built up to quite a climax on the Sunday afternoon." He punctuates the word *climax* with swirling arms.

I'm still puzzled. "So what?"

"Well, I would have had to leave the massage course early to go to my Mennonite choir practice," he replies, playing the innocent — a blank face and what-to-do shrug.

The woman at the box office leans over the table towards us. "Sorry to earwig, but *dat* was the best damn *ting* I heard all morning. G'bless you, sir."

~

It's been a year since Ireland became the world's first country to legalize gay marriage by popular vote, my dad reminds me when we're
back outside. On the one hand, it's surprising, in a country so recently
dominated by the Catholic Church, but these sorts of pendulum
swings aren't uncommon. After Quebec's Quiet Revolution, when
the province took control of education from the Catholic Church,
liberal, secular values flourished quite quickly.

"Apparently, there is a drag queen who's had a popular bingo
show on Irish primetime television for almost fifteen years," he
says casually.

I have stopped walking.

I must — must — hear that sentence again.

"A *drag queen* with a primetime *bingo show*," my dad confirms.

I have started walking. Quickly. Because we must — must — find
a café with wifi immediately. *Must* see this bingo show.

And after some searching and ordering of beverages neither of
us particularly wants, Holy Mary and Josephine, we find it.

The episode of *Telly Bingo* that comes up using the search words
drag queen bingo Ireland introduces us to Shirley Temple Bar, who has
been *calling the balls* for the National Lottery since 2001. Just need
to repeat that: the *National Lottery*. As far as drag queens go, she's
one of the more modest, almost school-girlish, dressed in a simple
black blouse with a pink bow at the neck and long, straight brown
hair. She has a both-rows-of-teeth showbiz smile, which she wears
constantly, even while speaking.

"And how's the weather there in County Clare, Sandra?" Shirley
asks a contestant who has called in to play a bonus tic-tac-toe game at
the top of the show. "Not too bad, Shirley," says Mrs. Creamer. The
two talk about weather, the rain, Mrs. Creamer's job as a personnel
manager. "So if I ever want a job, I know where to go," says Shirley
playfully, giving a flaring smile to the camera.

And then, well, it's bingo.

"That's *I*-two-and-five, number twenty-five," Shirley tells her viewers, who are presumably filling out some sort of bingo card at home. "And again an *I* with a seven, number seventeen. And that's a *B* on its own, the number one."

It is legendarily boring.

"I guess the transcendent part is when you win fifty thousand euros," my dad says, finishing his water and standing up. "Look, we've got to go. There's a lot of material I want to get through today, and we're running out of days."

"Hang on, it says she hosts live bingo at Dublin's largest gay bar every Thursday night . . . Wait . . . that's tonight! Dad, we have to go!"

He considers for a moment. "But we'll be at *Erect but Unstable,*" he says, sounding equal parts disappointed and relieved.

While he is lining up to pay for our drinks, I check my email. Because I can. And because I have developed the wretched habit of checking it whenever there is an opportunity. There is nothing earth-shattering or life-changing or pressing, at all, what a surprise, except that — wait — there's a response from the Move 4 Parkinson's people.

> Alison: Delighted to have you and your dad attend. Can you let me have his name. We encourage family members to join. Would love to have you come along. Look forward to meeting you. Mags

I look up, eager to tell my dad. He is still at the counter, the next in line. I watch him pull his credit card from his wallet and then watch the card fall, along with all of his other cards, onto the floor beside him. A clattering of plastic to which everyone in the vicinity responds kindly, bending down from counters and tables to pick everything up and return it to his grateful, shaking hands.

I look down and reread the email. Suddenly unsure about the whole thing.

Something I've noticed since we've been here is how little attention my dad gives any of this. In fact, I'm not sure he's mentioned the word Parkinson's since we arrived or brought the subject up on his own. In five days, I have yet to hear a word of complaint or frustration or self-pity or worry. Even when his tremors are severe and disruptive, he just tucks the hand in his pocket or behind him and carries on. He doesn't seem to want to pay it any notice at all.

I feel strangely awkward, as if I'm trying to spotlight something he would prefer to look beyond. As if I've gone behind his back by writing to this group without telling him. Have I? We walk several blocks before I find the courage to bring it up.

"Have you ever heard that dancing is very good for people with Parkinson's?"

He looks down as he speaks. "No, I hadn't heard that, but I think any kind of exercise is good."

I can feel myself moving around the subject delicately. "Yes, but I read something about how dancing can be especially helpful, something about the brain being stimulated in unusual ways when we combine movement with music."

"Well, isn't that interesting. I wonder if all my playing makes a difference," he says, referring to the hours he spends daily at the piano.

"Oh, I'm sure it does . . ."

"Yes, I actually find that when I sit down first thing in the morning and play for a few hours, it sort of *sets* something for the day." He motions the playing of a large chord on a keyboard. "Everything seems a bit better when I begin the day that way."

"Do you know the neurologist and writer Oliver Sacks?"

He shakes his head. "No, I don't think I do."

"Oh, you must look him up! I once heard him speak about how musical therapy was absolutely crucial for Parkinsonian patients because it can really release them. He tells an incredible story about a woman who was a great fan of Chopin, especially that Fantaisie . . ."

". . . in F-minor."

"Yes, I guess so. Anyway, she was unable to move or speak at this point, but if she was brought to a piano she could play that Chopin Fantaisie. And Oliver Sacks discovered that if he said the name of the piece, or even just the opus number . . ."

"Forty-nine."

"Is it? Okay, so even if someone just said to her *Opus 49*, this would stimulate a mental playing of the piece and she would be able to move normally for exactly the time it would take to play the piece. And then the moment it was over, she would become frozen again."

My dad is watching his feet as we walk. "Isn't that amazing."

"I know, isn't it? And of course no one really knows why music has that kind of effect, but apparently dancing can be just as liberating."

"Well, maybe I should try it."

I try to sound casual. "Actually, I was looking online and there's a group called Move 4 Parkinson's here in Dublin. They have a dance class on Fridays and they just sent me an email saying we'd be welcome to drop in."

He walks a few steps before replying. "Oh. Isn't that incredible," he says flatly.

We walk a few more steps in silence. The sidewalk narrows. He walks ahead.

"We'd go together . . ." I say, though that's obvious.

More silent walking.

"That would be tomorrow," he says over his shoulder.

"Yes, at two o'clock, I think," I say, reaching for my phone out of habit, nervousness, crutch. I want so much to do this together.

"But that will be our last full day to do research . . ."

My chest deflates. "Oh, yes, I guess it is, but it's in the afternoon . . ."

He walks a few paces, then turns around, his face bright. "Say, did I mention that I've had an email from a distant cousin in Louisiana? We think we might be related on the Egan side . . ."

I smile, drop my phone into my purse, let go of the whole idea.

NATIONAL LIBRARY

I am back at the beloved microfilm machines, completing the task that had my father nearly screaming yesterday, scanning family trees from the 1700s and watching for the names Thompson and Egan.

With every advance of the film, I imagine the names settling into suspenseful focus and the triumphant moment: *Dad! Here it IS!*

He's growing tenser as our chances of making the grand discoveries he had hoped for diminish by the day, the hour, but I have not given up hope. On the contrary, I keep building it up.

Dad! Here it IS!

It makes the task more exciting when I set up each viewing this way, so I begin to silently chant this mantra with every turn of the dial.

Dad! Here it IS!

But it never is.

My dad is bent over a long book with thick, heavy pages. He has one eye closed, as he often does when he is having trouble focusing, his face only inches from the parchment.

I do not disturb him. Instead, I return the reels to the front desk and ask if there is anything else for Wearing.

"Are you a bit on the chilly side?" the woman asks, puzzled.

I laugh. "No-no, anything else for *Joseph* Wearing? Any other materials?"

The woman blushes, apologizes, searches below the counter. She pulls up a small book — *Ballymote and the Parish of Emlaghfad* — and tells me it's all that's left. I creak it over to my dad's desk and settle in beside him. He doesn't look up. I crack the cover and read for a while until — "Uh!"

People look over at me, including my startled father.

"Sorry, just something . . . a tickle in my throat . . ."

He returns to his book, I to mine.

But I am terribly, terribly excited by this paragraph.

It's so clear, so affirming. My eyes leap and flit as I reread it:

> *The early historians of Ireland were drawn from the bardic schools and in the execution of their office did not always preserve the distinction between the recording and the celebrating of an event or epoch. Thus one finds a veil of exaggeration thrown over the lives of our most illustrious kings and heroes of this period which makes them more heroes of romance than reality. The stories which make up the cycle of Fionn and his Fianna, though tinged with a most vivid colouring, give more solid historical information than the airy and spiritless annals which later became the sources of Irish history.*

I want to jump up and down.

Because isn't it just so true. These annals we're all paging through, these census lists and parish records, aren't actually solid historical information at all. They look like facts, appear organized and definitive, but obviously they are also rife with human error, not to mention human nature, and they could only ever be as factual as the time and church allowed. Bastard children (as they were termed) were not uncommon, I've learned, and to spare the "fallen women" (as they were known), as well as the child and the entire family from condemnation, repudiation, and the fallout that comes of committing a grievous sin for which no length of atonement is ever sufficient (if you're a woman), these babies were often passed off and publicly registered as children of someone else: the grandparents, an aunt, a married sibling of the fallen daughter — that sort of post-natal sleight of hand.

Chambermaids and other women in service became pregnant by the men they served, though these men often denied their paternity and — can't you just hear them — scoffed at the very notion. One of the bastards in our own family was apparently the son of a chambermaid of Edward VII, a man infamous for cavorting. She insisted that her son's father was the king and the boy *did* grow into the spitting image of Edward VII, but who really knows?

Basically, people had sex and children all over the place, then as they do now. Names were misspelled, misheard, incorrectly entered, changed entirely, there were mistakes and omissions in registries and in the copying of records, and legions of people existed and procreated and were never registered at all. So, it's safe to assume that all family trees have fictional elements of one kind or another, no matter what it says on the actual birth certificates, how assiduous the research has been, and how sure the researcher might be that *that sort of thing* didn't go on in *their sort of family*. Because if *their sort of family* had human beings in it, chances are very good that *that sort of thing* went on.

So, as my new favourite book, *Ballymote and the Parish of Emlaghfad*, suggests, these "factual documents" are no more reliable as containers of history than fables, legends, tales, and yarns that speak to us in metaphor, paint full and imperfect portraits, point to possibilities and questions, and bring us closer to a greater understanding of the truth of the time. Removing the spirit and personal colouring from a story does not make it any more true, for it denies the very truth of human life: that it is messy, complicated, wild and flawed, mysterious and ultimately unknowable.

I'm in the middle of an epiphany. I am in full ascent, raising my mental fist towards a pinnacle of understanding on the nature of story, of truth, of life itself, when I feel my father looking over at me. I turn to him and simper.

"What are you finding?" he whispers.

I stir my hand around in the air, a move directly borrowed from the man asking the question. "It's speaking . . . in generalities . . . about the reading of history . . ."

He returns to the pages in front of him without saying a word.

I stop stirring. Close the book. *This is it*, I think, tapping the cover.

"There's nothing here," he says, closing his folder and crossing a few things off his master list. "We've exhausted the possibilities at this place, but there are still the manuscripts to get to!" He glances up at the clock, looks anxious.

∽

We walk quickly to the other end of the block. A far cry from the National Library Reading Room with its magnificent dome of vaulted light and frieze of dancing not-cherubs, the National Library *Manuscripts* Reading Room is the less attractive sibling. It's a fine room but plain, modern, with a wall of tall windows and spacious desks fitted with puffy pillows where fragile books and manuscripts can be nestled and consulted without any harm coming to their spines. It's a thoughtful space, relaxing, and ultimately more inter-esting beyond the surface, as the less attractive sibling often is.

The research I have been dispatched to do here has been both flavourless and maddening, a bit like chewing on a bulrush — something I have done only once before, at about age seven, when it took me only one large mouthful and a few chews to conclude that there were happier snacks to be had. I'd imagined it would taste like chocolate.

I've been looking through the estate papers of someone with one of those appalling hereditary titles the British Crown loved to award to keep the local savages under the control of one of their minions. Baron Ellis of Boyle in the County of Roscommon's estate papers comprise title deeds, receiving rentals, temporary rentals, rent rolls, wage receipts, estate valuations, accounts and vouchers, marriage and testamentary material, indentures and agreements, labour accounts and bills, and — my preferred section thus far — Use of Turf Banks and Fence Repairs.

I move on to a file of birth records.

1702 Novr 3rd Sarah daughter of Albert Nisbet Esq.

1702 March 22nd Margaret daughter of Mr. James Collins

1703 April 11th Robert son of Duke Giffard Esq.

1703 Aug 15th Garret son of William Tyrrel

"I guess these babies all came out of their fathers' bodies," I mutter to my dad, who looks up from his own manuscript across the table.

"You mean there's no mention of the mothers? Well, that's just the way . . . you know, patriarchy . . ." he says, waving airily and returning to his manuscript.

I love that summary and decide to adopt it whenever I'm at a loss to explain an incidence of sexism, misogyny, inequity in general.

You know, patriarchy . . . [airy wave]

And yes, of course I *know*, but it is still astonishing to see it penned as though the babies emerged, cleanly and sensibly, from their father's penises. I try to imagine the brazen entitlement of those men, sauntering down to the registry while their wives lay at home, expired and drenched with a newborn suckling at swollen breasts and four or five other kids running around them, women wholly unacknowledged, without rights to property, money, decent employment . . . you know, patriarchy . . .

> We therefore the said Judges upon due Examination and Consideration of the Premises do hereby declare and adjudge that the said Child was born a Bastard, upon the Body of the said Esther Waring.

There are only so many sentences like that I can read before the bulrush-in-the-mouth feeling becomes unbearable, hairy sand all over my tongue, my throat, the alphabetic equivalent of a hairball and its attendant urge to cough-retch until the vile wad is expelled.

We've been here for almost three hours and were in the main reading room for two before that, but my father is showing no signs of flagging, no fatigue at all, in fact, still no need for lunch, tea, a snack, a rejuvenating walk around St. Stephen's Green, a look at an exhibit in the main lobby on Ireland's participation in World War I, though I have suggested each of those activities.

I take a break on my own. A sip of water at the fountain in the hallway, a wander to the lockers for a mint, a jaw-wag with the security guard, who walked into his job one day after the economic crash only to learn that his salary had been cut by a turd (one-third) and it's never been raised back up again, and a chat with the guys at the library counter, who are terrific: friendly and helpful and happy to chew the fat about all manner of nonsense — Canadian weather, American primaries — while helping people order manuscripts from the shelves below ground.

"When was it," the older of the two men asks me, leaning on the counter as if it were a bar and there were a bottle between us rather than the Church of Ireland Registers for the Diocese of Meath. "When was it that everything that used to be a sin became a virtue?" I tell him I'm not sure.

"Ambition, avarice — they're all celebrated now, aren't they? They're what you need to be a politician, to get ahead, it seems. I'll never understand why we celebrate in our leaders qualities that we wouldn't put up with in our own children. That's some kind of collective madness, so it is."

I agree that it is.

"And the United States of America has to be the maddest place on Earth at present, isn't it? This election, it's nothing but a vulgar reality television show. That one's got a face like a bulldog chewing a wasp!"

I jot that phrase onto a slip of paper and fold it into my back pocket. The man looks pleased.

"But Canada!" he says, raising his index finger. "Now there's a place with a bit of sanity about it at last. You're lucky, being Canadian. Though, for the record, the moment you walked in here this morning, I knew I was looking at an Irish girl."

Which is a very funny thing. Because I am brown-eyed with brown curly hair that has such a mind of its own it should probably have its own driver's licence. Far from the typical blue-eyed, red-haired Irish lass.

"Hardly . . ." I say, holding up a handful of dark curls.

To which our man straightens up. "Ah, but there you have it! Your family hails from the west country, isn't it?"

I remind him that he has been helping me pull up documents from western parishes all afternoon.

"Right you are and no mistake," he says, leaning closer and lowering his voice. "But if you were to indulge me a moment, I'd be delighted to bring to your attention a chapter of Irish history that will go lengths to explain how the locks you hold in your hand have their origins in a shipwreck of the Spanish Armada."

I *live* for sentences like that.

If I could pull a bottle out of my purse and pour us two glasses, I would, so I mime the decanting of an imaginary bottle and, being a good sport, our man — Callum, for if we are to be drinking together, it seems right that we call each other by name — reaches for one of the invisible glasses, raises it, and says *cheers*, before running a hand over his comb-over and leaning both arms on the library counter.

"Now, I don't know your level of knowledge concerning the Spanish Armada," Callum starts, raising a hand in a gesture of apology, pardon.

"I think it would be Level One," I say, to which he nods and lowers his hand.

"So you might well be aware of the large fleet of ships dispatched from Spain in 1588 with the purpose of invading England. And you'll know that following a crushing defeat in the English Channel, what remained of the one-hundred-and-thirty-strong fleet was forced up to the North Sea in retreat."

I am nodding, though I suspect I'm actually Level Zero.

"Now, many of the ships that survived the battle sustained serious damage from the gunships — structural damage, of course, but also damage to navigational equipment — and they were not at all fit for the conditions of the North Atlantic! As fate would have it, after sailing their way past the Orkneys and the Hebrides, the ships met with ferocious storms that blew the fleet dramatically off course and right" — Callum drives one hand hard onto the counter — "into the rocky shores of western Ireland." He tsks and shakes his head. "About two dozen ships were wrecked, they figure, and more than a thousand men drowned. Oh, if you'll excuse me a moment . . ."

A woman has approached the desk with a written request for materials. Callum greets her by name, files her request, exchanges a few well-wishes, and returns to my end of the counter. Waits a moment until the woman has reached the far side of the room, then whispers, "That woman's grandfather was a great hero of Ireland: Thomas MacDonagh, a poet, one of the leaders of the Easter Rising." He lowers his voice further. "Executed by firing squad at Kilmainham Gaol. Nasty business. You'll see his face on plaques and posters all over Dublin at the moment."

I glance over at the woman, in her late sixties or seventies perhaps, and watch as she straightens the sleeves of her cardigan and settles in at the table next to my dad. I consider going over and slipping him a note — *granddaughter of one of executed leaders of Easter Rising sitting next to you!* — but I decide not to distract him. Or alert him to the fact that I am brushing up on the Spanish Armada.

"Now, sorry, where did I leave you . . ." Callum mutters, probing his forehead with his fingertips, as if he might physically find the spot.

"On the rocky west coast of Ireland."

He leaps to life. He actually leaps, though not far. "So it was. Treacherous! The rocks chewed those ships to bits! Hundreds of men lost at sea. But" — he pauses, raises a finger — "for a two-mile stretch of sand at the strand of Streedagh, County Sligo, where three of the ships were blown ashore. And where" — he pauses again, finger still raised — "thanks only to that soft and forgiving sand, a number of the crew from *those* ships did manage to survive."

I can see where this story is going.

"And what you'll find" — he is leaning even closer now, his smile is like a string of lights across his face — "in that part of Ireland is quite a number of people with dark eyes and curly brown hair just like yours," he concludes, setting his fist down firmly on the counter to make his case complete. "And there's no shame in it, none at all. The Spanish were good friends and allies of the Irish people, so they were," he says, winking and stepping away from the counter.

His suggestion is both ludicrous and fabulous. Not only for the romantic quality of it — shipwrecked Spaniards flung up on a beach in County Sligo! — and not only because it is the first plausible explanation I've ever had of the dark sheep's wool that grows on my head. But the most absurd, almost eerie, thing about this story is that I have always had a passionate, verging on obsessive, affinity for all things Spanish.

Learning the language was like finding a lost glove and slipping it on. It was that effortless, that familiar and comforting — like a song I'd known in childhood whose lyrics were distant but easily recalled. Spanish music brings me to my knees, always has. And nowhere do I feel less foreign than in the company of Spanish-speaking people. My partner and I ended up raising our son in Mexico, and leaving that country to return to Canada felt like an amputation.

I'm losing sight of logic, grasping at straws, masts of the sunken Spanish Armada, but there is so much about this story that makes visceral, intuitive sense to me. It may be right up there with *perhaps my great-great-grandfather's being a blacksmith explains my affinity for metalwork*, but maybe that's not such a half-crazed notion either. In fact, it's entirely in keeping with the concept of genetic memory, that our genes are carriers not only of physical traits but psychological ones as well: memories, knowledge, intuitive responses, and traumas.

After spending the week dissing all things genealogical, suddenly I find myself wondering if there might be something to this stuff after all.

∿

With good reason, perhaps, my father has grown weary of my eureka moments as regards our research. To allay his suspicions of insincerity, therefore, I make an effort to tone down my excitement.

"Dad," I whisper, sneaking a quick glance at Thomas MacDonagh's granddaughter on my way to my father's worktable. She is poring over a thick stack of parchments, but I can't make out what they are. "Dad, I've just had an interesting conversation with one of the librarians and he has a theory about our origins."

My dad looks up. Blank. He's either exhausted or uninterested. Possibly both.

As calmly as I can, I recount the Spanish Armada saga (!), the survivors who were flung onto a sandy beach in County Sligo (!), the possible answer to the Wearing Family Curls mystery (!).

My father's own hair is also of the steel-wool variety, though he has kept it closely shaven for decades. "You mean that we're what's known as Black Irish," he says casually. "That's a term sometimes used to describe Irish people with dark eyes and dark hair like ours. They are competing theories, but some of them suggest a connection to Spain, yes . . ." he says, already returning to his manuscript.

"But Dad," I whisper insistently, "it explains *everything*."

"I'm going to be through here in a minute," he says. "And then I have one more volume to go. Maybe you could just finish with those birth records."

I tuck my wagging tail between my legs, banish all thoughts of armadas and flotillas of any kind, and plough through the rest of the birth records. But now, when I stumble over a phrase like *the said Child was born a Bastard upon the Body of the said Esther Waring*, I don't feel outrage so much as curiosity as to how many of these women might have had rolls on the beach with descendants of the you-know-what. Entries such as *1703 Aug 15th Garret son of William Tyrrel* now set me to wondering how many of these proud fathers might have marched down to register newborn babes they assumed to be their own, only to puzzle later over the children's strange wiry black curls, their piercing brown eyes, so unlike anyone else in the family and so much like those strangers whose forefathers washed ashore after battle.

I am inventing stories as quickly as my eyes are scanning the pages, members of the Spanish Armada are washing up around me every time I turn a page. It may not be genealogy in the strictest sense — it may not be genealogy at all — but whatever it is, it gets the job done.

~

"Your other files have arrived," Callum tells me when I heave the last of the birth records to the counter.

"*Other* files?"

I must have squeaked the words, broadcast a look of terror, for Callum rushes to put his hand on my arm, as if to steady me, and quickly clarifies: "The ones you asked to be delivered towards the end of the day."

I exhale so fully I almost fold in half. "Oh, *those*."

He looks more amused than alarmed. "It looks thin," he says of the file folder, aiming to be kind. "You should be through it in no time at all."

I smile, wearily, take the folder to the nearest table, and sit down. Do a few eyebrow push-ups, give my cheeks a few soft wake-up whacks, and open the file.

The first thing I notice is the image of a peacock.

Then:

MYNGOON-MIN
Prince
Héritier de Birmanie
90 Rue Legrand de la Linaye
Saigon

19th November 1909

Sir,

I am desired by H.R.H. The Prince Héritier de Birmanie to convey His Highness' thanks for your weekly papers known as the "The Gaelic American" which was sent by post and duly received by the Prince.

As His Highness also likes to hear your arguments in your paper, I have the honour to enclose herewith two ($2.00) in Notes as subscription to your papers which will be mailed regularly to us, for 1/2 year.

I believe you should know about the circumstances of the Prince, who is the only legitimate and eldest inheritor of Burma now under the British flag. The Prince will create the New Movement to drive the Alienate governments away from Burma whose people have sustained wrongful loss of their property at the hands of the British, and the Burmese Buddhists desire the Prince to be their Ruler, owing to the torment and tyranny of the merciless government.

I request on behalf of the Prince, in conclusion, that you will accept my cordial congratulations upon your actions for the freedom of Ireland and sincere thanks for your sympathy with the Indian Nations together with my best wishes for your welfare and prosperity.

I have the honour to be, Sir,
Your most obedient servant
[signature]
Private Secretary to HRH
the Prince d'B

I know nothing of Burmese history, nothing of the Prince d'B, but I love the idea of His Royal Majesty Mingoon-Min subscribing to the *Gaelic American* while (presumably) in exile in Saigon. And the thought of his taking inspiration from Irish freedom movements as the British stomped through his own country confiscating whatever property they damn well pleased — *you know, imperialism . . . [airy wave]* — makes me lean back in my seat and try to map all of that out.

I get only so far.

In fact, I get only as far as Saigon (now Ho Chi Minh City) and memories of the last time I saw Tasha, when she was living in Vietnam. I had come to spend a month tootling around the country, using Tasha's home in Hanoi as a base. I thought *tootle* was the perfect verb for the trip, as I was travelling with my son, then a toddler, and I thought tootling with a toddler down the length of that thin and fascinating country, from Hanoi to Ho Chi Minh, would make for a wonderful time and, perhaps, even a wonderful book.

I pictured toddling around temples, pagodas, and markets; afternoons spent in parks filled with local children playing and laughing, my son happily among them, effortlessly absorbing Vietnamese while I sat at a gentle distance and wrote about the day's adventures. Filled page after page. Peacefully inserted motherhood into my career as a travel writer, which had been somewhat stalled since the birth.

There is no need to report the news that said book did not get written. That said park with a band of merry and obliging playmates was never located. And that there was virtually no tootling of any kind, because a toddler is not interested in travelling the length of thin and fascinating countries, he is interested in practising new skills: running, ideally into traffic; climbing up and down stairs, with assistance, ideally hundreds of times; and stalwartly outgrowing the nap.

In four weeks, I wrote seven words: *What were you thinking you fucking moron.* The rest of the month, I focused on scooping my son out of the way of traffic (the quaint Asian variety that finds itself on the sidewalks as often as on the roads), climbing the steps to Ho Chi Minh's tomb over and over and over and over and over and over, and taking extensive tours of parking lots, as my son was endlessly delighted by the assessing, touching, admiring, and mounting of all the things Vietnamese that went VROOM. I tried other things — palaces, temples, museums — but they were calamitous, incongruous outings. A bit like taking a ferret to a yoga class. So we spent our days in active examination of vehicles in various Vietnamese cities whose names are utterly irrelevant, the one exception being the city of Hué, a UNESCO World Heritage site and the capital of unified Vietnam under the Nguyen Dynasty from 1802 to 1945. Every toddler should go. For one thing, there is a walled citadel within which there is no traffic, and for another, the street markets sell very cheap knock-off Lego, similar to the name-brand stuff but for the negligible detail that the bricks do not actually fit together. The parking lots, though, are genuine and remarkable.

By the time I met up with Tasha at the end of our journey, I had lost fifteen pounds and most of my mental capacities.

∾

I request permission from Callum to take a couple of pictures of the Burmese prince's letter for Tasha, log into the library's internet, and send the photos — *whoosh* — to Cambridge, along with a quick note. *Wish you were here. The traffic is lovely.*

∾

At last, my father is ready to go. He's been at it, non-stop, for almost seven straight hours, but somehow he doesn't even look tired.

I press the button for the elevator. "What's your secret, Dad? Where do you get your stamina?"

The doors open.

My dad says *passion* as though it were the password to get into the elevator and steps in. "Now," he continues, as the doors are closing, "let's go find a pub."

NASSAU STREET

It's called rain, but it's actually layers of the atmosphere being sloughed from the sky, entire weather systems sliding onto the sidewalks, sweeping across the roads. We duck into the first place we find, though it is the antithesis of an Irish pub. It's a restaurant, pricey and precious, and the waiter is stuffy and dismissive. He is either a Frenchman who has lived in Ireland a long time or an Irishman faking a French accent. We stand at the entrance trying to decide what to do, until the rain begins to pelt the door of the restaurant horizontally and my dad says, "Oh, let's just go in," and we do.

The waiter settles us into high-backed wicker chairs and hands us menus that are fashionably unreadable, full of reductions and essences, pasta shapes I've never heard of, things I assume are rare smoked meats, and dishes like Miso-Glazed Wood Pigeon with Fennel Jam & Ponzu. It's not really the place for a pint of Guinness, so my dad orders a bottle of champagne to celebrate . . . something . . . and goes to find the washroom.

While he is gone, I add, *The Way He Celebrates Nothing in Particular,* *the Day, Whatever.* Plus *His Sherry-Bread Scent,* because I forgot to write that one down the other day.

When my father returns, our waiter uncorks the bottle discreetly into a thick napkin and does the standard pour-and-wait-for-nod formality, before pouring tall glasses of bubbly.

"To our fourth day of research!" my dad chirps.

"And to the Spanish Armada!" I add.

I can tell from his vacant chuckle that my dad has forgotten all about my discovery, but he says, "Oh yes, hooray for the armada!" and toasts them anyway. We were planning to just have a pint and cook dinner at home, but because of the rain my dad suggests we just settle in and eat here.

When the waiter deigns to visit us again, I order something called Raz el Hanout & Garden Carrot Symphony to which my dad says, "Oh, I think Michael and I heard a performance of that last year," before selecting the risotto with preserved truffle, foraged mushrooms, tonka beans, and hippo tops.

"How could I resist that?" he asks the waiter, who does not find any of this funny at all. When the food arrives, it does so in keeping with the trendy proportion of food to crockery: miniscule portions on gargantuan plates. My carrot symphony is more of a chamber ensemble. Dad's risotto could fit in the palm of his hand, but it sits in a bowl that looks like the helmet of a Mongolian warrior. I ask the waiter to point out the hippo tops, which I'd assumed were a rare and exotic mushroom but which are, in fact, "a species of ze watercress," the waiter tells us wearily, as if I'd asked him to please sing us some French nursery rhymes while we eat. It's delicious, all four bites of it, and then it's time for dessert, which neither of us normally orders but which is essential if we want to make it to the next block without having to stop for fish and chips.

My dad suggests ordering one Frozen Nyangbo Chocolate Mousse with Crab Pear & Tahitian Vanilla and one Opalys

Chocolate Bavarois with Wild Blackberry & Lime and seeing which one is better! His eyes actually do a little can-can at this idea, while the waiter raises his own eyes to the ceiling.

There's no one else in the entire restaurant. There was an American couple sitting by the window when we arrived and a table of boisterous young men, a couple of them French, talking about a car race, but the place has been empty ever since.

My dad's arm has been shaking throughout the meal, but as we are dividing the desserts, his cutlery begins banging so loudly against his plate that the waiter walks over and cranes his head, trying to see the source of the racket. I look over at him, and from the warm and understanding smile he offers me in return, it's clear I've misjudged him.

Maybe he's an Irishman faking the accent after all.

"Is it getting much worse, would you say?" I ask, watching the wide circles my dad's arm makes above his plate.

"A bit . . . Well, it depends. It's worse when I'm tired," he says, reaching for his champagne glass with his good hand and lifting it as a prop. "And better when I drink alcohol."

"Really? Or is that a good excuse?"

He laughs. "No-no, apparently that's quite common for people with Parkinson's." He takes a sip with his steady hand. "*And* it's a nice excuse."

"But it does seem to be quite slow-moving." I can feel myself clinging to that statement as I say it. I've seen people with advanced Parkinson's, the rigidity and laboured gait, the gradual self-imprisoning. "Very slow-moving," I repeat, willing the statement into being.

He nods. "Yes, my doctor's said that. And the drugs seem to help." He adjusts his napkin. "Until they wear off." He looks up and smiles gently.

We both do.

"It's too bad the dancing is tomorrow," he says, taking another sip of champagne. "It might have been possible on the weekend, but we still need to get to the Representative Church Body Library and it's only open on weekdays. And we also need to go back to the Registry of Deeds . . ." He reaches for his notebook — he is forever reaching for his notebook, the same way people check their phones — and begins flipping the pages forcefully, tapping his finger on a couple of notes, resting his forehead on his hand, sighing. I can't bear to watch how frustrated he is, how worried he is that we might not find anything. That all of the questions he has come with might remain unanswered.

I've known all along how much all of this means to him, yet I haven't *felt* how much this means to him until just now. Suddenly, I can't believe how lightly I've been taking all of this, how much time I've wasted joking around, taking breaks, taking the piss out of it all while my poor dad slogs away. It's appalling how little I've invested, the paltry efforts I've put into this endeavour. I want to tip backwards and claim some lost time, go back and begin this again with more devotion, a degree of seriousness, an honest commitment. "I'm so sorry, Dad. I'm afraid I haven't been any help at all. You've put so much into this week and we're coming away with nothing. I hope this isn't my fault . . ."

He reaches over and pats my arm. "Now, now, don't blame yourself. You've been a wonderful help. And you know how damn complicated it all is. As you've said yourself, most of what I'm looking for probably doesn't even exist, so it's a bit like looking for a needle in a haystack — when you're not even sure the needle is there to begin with."

By the time we're back outside, the rain is forgotten history, the sky clanging with sunshine. "Why don't we take a walk around Merrion Square before we head back to Smithfield?" he suggests.

"We have a distant relative who used to work on Merrion Square. One of the Egans."

I'm not sure if it's dehydration or the size of my Garden Carrot Symphony relative to the bottle of champagne we just drained or some residual thrill from the Spanish Armada connection or what it is, but I feel completely and unabashedly sloshed. My limbs are dancing beneath me. I keep saying *hi!* to people as they pass us on the sidewalk, including a young man leaning against a lamppost smoking a cigarette. He doesn't return my smile. Instead, he begins trailing a young couple, somewhat suspiciously, I feel, so I begin wandering through every possible explanation of what he might be up to when my dad clutches my arm and says, "Oh, look, it's Oscar Wilde!"

He is outstretched on a rock, propped up on his elbows and observing the world in a fashionable forest-green jacket with deep-pink quilted cuffs and trim. He cups a pipe in his right hand, squints. If Shirley were here, she'd say, *WELL, AREN'T YOU JUST THE VISION OF DAPPER AND DANDY!*, but she isn't, so I say it in her place.

People are gathered around taking pictures. The sculpture is charming, gnomic, the coloured marble fitting for a man so elegantly colourful in life and wit. I take a few photos of my dad next to the statue and then we take turns reading from two marble pillars onto which some of Wilde's most famous aphorisms have been engraved.

Be yourself. Everyone else is taken.

Who, being loved, is poor?

Lying, the telling of beautiful untrue things, is the proper aim of art.

The truth is rarely pure and never simple.

I take issue with Wilde over the last two quotes, arguing that the truth may not be simple, but it is pure.

"Oscar Wilde did pride himself on being provocative," my dad reminds me.

"Yeah, I guess so," I reply. And normally, I'd leave it at that. But I'm tipsy, a bit punchy, so I feel compelled to start philosophizing about how pure truth actually is. How it is a somatic state, something that can only be experienced, crucially different from facts, which point the way to truth but which cannot ever fully express it.

"Don't you agree, Dad?"

He says yes, but in a placating tone that makes me suspect he actually doesn't. And then he wishes, aloud, that he had the exact address of the distant Egan relative on Colon's side of the family. All he knows is that he worked somewhere on Merrion Square. Maybe over there . . .

And perhaps it is the absurdity of that particular mission, or the champagne-to-carrot-symphony ratio, or a lifetime of feeling intellectually inferior, or a swirling psychic soup of all of those factors, but whatever it is, I am now hell-bent on making my case for truth in such a way that my dad will see my point.

As we walk in search of god-knows-which-relative's possible former office for god-knows-what purpose, I circle back on the subject, this recurring schism: my dad's devotion to academic methods, logic, and cold, hard facts set against my own devotion to intuition, gut instinct, and passionately probable invention; my dad's conviction that the truth can be located within facts, pinned down, proven, and footnoted, set against my equally stubborn conviction that facts are only steps in the direction of truth, which seems almost numinous in nature. I can hear myself getting louder, but I cannot seem to rein myself in. I try to explain the epiphany I had this morning while reading that book in the National Library.

"Hang on, I made some notes . . ." I fumble through my purse, my journal, shepherd my eyes towards the page. "The basic idea was how the early Irish historians were bards, poets, and . . . okay, here it is . . . the classic myths, *though tinged with a most vivid colouring, give more solid historical information than the spiritless annals which later became the sources of Irish history.*"

I look over at my dad and can tell, simply by his profile, how unexcited he is by this suggestion. Not that he isn't a fan of poetry and myth, but spiritless annals have been our raison d'être these last four days. They are the reason we are in Ireland.

"Well, like it or not, reliable history is an assemblage of facts, not poetic stories," he declares, shutting me down.

One of the great benefits of growing older and more comfortable and accepting of oneself is how much easier it becomes to Just Let Things Go. Comments that might have elicited a fierce reaction in a younger self can now be left to echo into silence where they belong. Circular arguments can be avoided, egos and feelings may be spared, harmony and respect have the opportunity to reign. But clearly a bottle of champagne poured over a petite lunch has a way of regressing a person, because I can feel myself discarding whatever maturity, wisdom, and evolution I've eked out over the last half century in favour of a flagrantly drunken lecture about how *right* about this I actually am.

"The only people who believe in history are those who are well represented by it . . ." I say and then pause to stand impressed at my own sentence. "Women, Indigenous people, the colonized — ask *them* about the power of omission and whether facts can just as easily be used to tell a false story as a truthful one."

My dad, being older than I, is even more practised in the art of Just Letting Things Go. He says nothing in response to the points I keep making but thinks he might have found the office on the southernmost corner of Merrion Square that fits the description Colon gave him. It would be that one over there.

"It's not that facts aren't essential, Dad. It's that they're incomplete. The truth of something as complex as human beings can never be expressed entirely through facts. It requires art and metaphor, colour and . . . and love. Let's say two people say *I love you*; one means it and the other doesn't. So the words are the same, but that's not where the truth resides, is it? It's more subtle than that. We know when we are in the presence of love not by the words themselves, but by the visceral echo of those words. *That's* where truth resides, don't you think? In that echo, that felt resonance?"

My dad lets a bit of time pass, a column of silence rise up around us. "I think you might have had more of the champagne than I did" is his quiet response.

Briefly, I'm miffed. Until I take a moment to notice how numb my lips are.

"Maybe we should try having this conversation again another time," he suggests as we reach the end of the park.

I know he's right — debates should never continue past the insensate stage — but I also feel muted, feel theories and arguments practically piling up in my throat.

He seems to notice. "I do want to hear what you have to say," he says, "and it's very interesting. But it's been quite a long day." He threads his arm through mine and leans his head on my shoulder. "So maybe you can just go easy on this old guy today?"

I tip my head against his — our curly hair rubs together for a moment — and we step back onto the streets of Dublin, arm in arm.

OUTHOUSE THEATRE

Erect but Unstable is terrific: well written and expertly performed. The series of stories is set in Montreal and detail the actor's coming to terms with his sexuality, a struggle that has taken most of his life. The sketches are as funny as they are heartbreaking, painfully hilarious scenes of a man grappling to understand himself through dialogues with conservative relatives, emotionally distant ex-lovers, an elementary school teacher, a rabbi. My dad is the most responsive member of the small audience, laughing loudly at every opportunity, applauding with all his might at the end.

Those antics used to humiliate me when I was a child, mortify me as a teenager: that unrestrained laughter — a giggle arpeggio that was conspicuous even in a noisy crowd, to say nothing of a silent theatre — and the way he would cup his hands in such a way that his applause practically burst the eardrums of the people around him, shouting *BRAVO! BRAVO!* after an excellent performance, even if he was the only person in the entire hall doing so.

I'm not sure at what point the baton was passed, as it were, and I became the person in the audience whose riotous laughter has been known to loosen up the rest of the audience. No doubt my son finds it as humiliating as I did. But perhaps he'll eventually carry on the tradition. It seems to be how these things go.

As we are leaving the theatre, the actor stands by the door and thanks all of us for coming. My dad overflows with loud and generous compliments before asking, "And can we assume the stories in the show were true?"

The actor smiles. "They're all imaginatively true. I changed the details that needed to be altered for the stories to work as theatre, of course, but they're all drawn from experience."

"Oh!" my dad exclaims, throwing his arms open in my direction. "You would get along well with my daughter!"

I feel a swell of protest, an impulse to explain the comment, but I don't. I'm too busy watching how the small crowd of people around us is watching my dad, his full-body enthusiasm, the way his arms conduct the air when he speaks and laughs, the occasional spray of spit as his face explodes with joy. It's infectious. People are smirking, exchanging cheerful glances with each other, with me, and it's family camp all over again — minus the choral satire and the garbage bag costumes, mind you, but with a similar twinkling elation.

I have the urge to wrestle time to a halt, cast a hard frame around this moment, and force it go on and on and on. Hold my dad this way forever.

But no sooner have I tried to freeze the moment than it is over, my dad is heading out of the theatre, the actor is talking to someone else, people are moving on.

∾

We wander back to Smithfield in a quiet rain.

"It's interesting to see how difficult it can still be for someone to come out, even when they live in a progressive city within a progressive country and surrounded by gay culture if they want to be," my dad says.

"Oh, I know!" I reply. "I was thinking the same thing."

"I think it's partly because despite all the advances, almost everyone still resists being part of a minority. I'm always struck, for instance, when Michael and I travel, how few gay people we see or recognize. When we return home, we move back into our sweet little gay lives, with our concert groups and friends and dinner parties and so on, and it's all normalized again, but every time I travel, I'm struck by it all over again."

I'm surprised to hear him use the term *minority*, hadn't known he thought in those terms.

"But it's amazing how much progress has been made in my lifetime," I say, thinking of my teenage son who mentions his gay grandfather to his friends without even blinking.

"Oh, *heavens*, yes!" my dad replies. He practically sings the word *heavens*. "I used to listen to the young guys in the swim club talking so casually about what they were going to do with their boyfriends on the weekend or the lunch they had with their boyfriend's mother or whatever, and I'd think, *You guys have no idea how easy you have it!*" He is speaking like an Italian, with bountiful gestures and booming pronouncements.

"But that's wonderful!" I counter, joining in on the Italian gesturing.

"Oh, yes, it *is* wonderful, of course. But once, I can't remember what we were talking about, but I mentioned the bath raids, and some of those young guys had never even heard of them! And okay, the raids were thirty years ago, but I was astonished to think that all that might have been forgotten already. Of course, I'm thrilled with all the rights and freedoms we have now, but I also feel strongly that we shouldn't take any of them for granted. One only has to think of Berlin in the '20s and '30s."

"Which was . . . ?"

"Oh, it had a thriving gay scene, with popular gay clubs and drag cabarets — even *straight* people would go! It was one of the safest and most accepting places in Europe for gay people." He presses the button for the crosswalk, stares straight ahead. "And then Hitler became chancellor."

∽

We're tired, both of us, once we are back at John's with our feet up, and the conversation is political and forgettable until my dad's casual mention of something *ringing true*.

"Yes, I love that expression — it *rings true* or it has *the ring of truth* — because it says so much about the nature of truth, don't you think? It's that resonance I was talking about earlier when I was all tanked up on bubbly."

He nods. Looks reluctant to start up the conversation again.

"I sometimes wonder if truth has an actual resonance," I offer.

"I'm not sure I know what you mean."

"Well, think of the act of coming out, being transparent and boldly, vulnerably honest. I remember you telling me when I was a teenager that it was as if an enormous weight had been lifted when you finally knew, and accepted, you were gay — despite the upheaval that same revelation was going to cause."

He takes a sip of wine. "Yes, that's right."

"So, why do you think that is, that truth has that quality of liberation to it?"

He shrugs. "Well, because it frees us from lies and deception and that sort of thing."

"Yes, but why is that liberating? Do you see what I'm asking? What is it about truth that is so freeing? Why wasn't it freeing to lie in such a way that you fit in with society? Wouldn't that have been easier, *less* of a burden?"

He pauses, looks down at his wineglass. "I have a feeling you're going to tell me . . ."

I sit up taller. "Well, actually, I think it's related to that concept of ringing true, that truth is an actual resonance or vibration that has a sort of purity about it, almost a healing quality. And that's why it can be such a visceral experience."

"Um-hm."

"It's as if truth actually tunes us, brings us into alignment some-how. I always tell people in my memoir classes that truth may cause pain, but it doesn't do damage the way deception does. We might believe, or tell ourselves, that keeping something secret will spare someone pain, and it might, in the short term, but ultimately, it's so insidious. Whereas truth, while it might be painful, really does set us free in the end, don't you think?"

My dad inhales deeply, leans back in his chair. "Well, I agree, in principle, but people have very different ideas of what the truth is. I don't think there's actually such a thing as Truth with a capital T."

"Well, yeah. I mean, no, wait. Of course everyone has their own perspective or version of something that happened, but truth and perspective aren't the same thing. The truth I'm talking about doesn't reside in the realm of events and opinions and who-actually-said-what and so on. It transcends all of that somehow, which is why it's so diffi-cult to pin down in words." I take a sip of wine, swallow quickly, and add, "It's ineffable."

My dad smiles sardonically. "Well, for something that is ineffable, you certainly manage to talk a lot about it."

I wince a small smile and sit quietly for a while. My dad begins looking through his notes. And it's such a familiar posture, this sitting and watching my dad read.

When we were kids, my brothers and I used to have contests to see who could break his concentration: we'd try arm-farting, real fart-ing, whispering swear words within earshot, claiming to see — hey, look! — a camel in the backyard. But even more fun than breaking his attention was having it, for he could be equally engrossed in something we did together, be it a game or an adventure or a crazy, made-up-on-the-spot song.

After he came out and moved to Toronto, his regard was considerably harder to come by. His new life was so colourful, so vibrant, so full of people who fascinated and attracted him, who continually pulled him out of our orbit and into theirs. Without realizing it, winning my dad's attention became my modus operandi, affecting my decisions and shaping my life well into adulthood. I used to wonder if, when a parent drifts from us at a young age, part of us is forever reaching for them. And if we ever stop.

~∽

I head to my bedroom and reach for Gustave de Beaumont's *Ireland.* Only when I glance again at the publication date — 1839 — do I realize that the author, who was a friend and travel companion to Alexis de Tocqueville (whose famous *Democracy in America* was published about the same time), would have been in Ireland conducting his research precisely as my ancestors were leaving the country and that this book is, therefore, a sketch of the very Ireland they inhabited.

Even then, famine was an annual occurrence largely ignored and underplayed by the British. In 1835, around the time the four families my dad and I have been researching left for Canada in hopes of a better life, the British government conducted an inquiry into social conditions in Ireland, which produced a 900-page report, *every page, line, and word of which establish Irish misery*, Beaumont writes, *but where, nevertheless, all the miseries of Ireland are not reported.*

> *The author of this book, to whom such evidence ought to have sufficed, still was anxious to see with his own eyes what his reason hesitated to believe. Twice, in 1835 and 1837, whilst travelling through Ireland, he visited the counties where*

*famine is accustomed to rage with most violence, and he veri-
fied the facts. Shall he relate what he saw? — No. There are
misfortunes so far beyond the pale of humanity, that human
language has no words to represent them. Besides, were he
to recal [sic] the scenes of sadness and desolation he has
witnessed; — to repeat the howlings and yells of despair he
has heard; — were he required to relate the anguishing tone
of a mother's voice refusing a portion of food to her famish-
ing children; — and if, in the midst of such extreme misery,
he were required to portray the insulting opulence which
the rich ostentatiously displayed to all eyes; — the magnificence of the lordly palace sustained by columns of the finest
marble from Greece or Italy, and which the gold of America,
the silks of France, and the tissues of India, vie to decorate;
— the splendid residence designed for servants, the still more
superb building destined for horses; — all the wonders of
art, all the inventions of industry, and all the caprices of
vanity, accumulated on a spot where the owner does not even
deign to reside, but makes his visits "few and far between;"
— the sumptuous and indolent life of the wealthy landlord,
who knows nothing of the misery of which he is the author;
— never has glanced at it; — does not believe its existence; —
draws from the sweat of the industrious poor his 20,000l. a
year — every one of whose senseless and superfluous luxuries
represents the ruin or destitution of some unfortunate being;
— who every day gives his dogs the food of a hundred families and leaves those to perish by hunger who support him in
this life of luxury and pride; — if the author of this book
were required to recal [sic] the sinister impressions produced
by such contrasts, and the terrible question which such appo-
sitions raised in his soul, he feels that the pen would fall from
his hands, and that he would not have courage to complete
the task which he has undertaken to accomplish.*

I let the book fall to my chest, the words thunder through me, then I roll out of bed and pad down the hall. "Hey, Dad."

He looks up from his notes.

"What if they were just miserable?"

He squints. "What if who was just miserable?"

"The four families we've been researching. I was reading your *Ireland* book and, my god, the 1830s was a wretched, atrocious time, with horrific disparity and destitution, and masses of people were starving even *before* the official beginning of the Great Famine. So what if their decision to leave Ireland was simply driven by a desire to flee a country where people were dying of starvation all around them and where there were almost no opportunities to improve their lives?"

"Um-hm," he says, looking back down at his notes. "But that's just speculation."

I stand for a moment and watch him cross-check some call numbers for the materials we'll be looking for tomorrow. Part of me wants to go back and grab the book, read the passage aloud, prove my theory, show him I have an interesting perspective, something valuable to add. I am about to act on the impulse, when something stops me. A desire to just stand here, observing him, seeing how much all this means to him, how much he cares. The sight softens me, settles me. And the longer I stand simply observing him, the less I feel a need to do anything else but that.

FRIDAY

10 BOW STREET

"Ultimately, there's no real way of knowing for sure, is there?" I ask.

My dad barely registers the question. "Know what?"

"Well, for example, somewhere along the line someone might have lied about an illegitimate child they had with someone who's not in any of these records and then that whole line of descendants is completely false. I mean, there's no real way of knowing if we're *actually* related to Thomas Egan or Henry Faunt or any of the rest of them, is there? We're just going by what's been written down, which may or may not be true."

He looks up. Looks crushed.

I feel beastly, rush to lighten the idea. "But does it really matter? I mean, can't we just engage with the story and its characters as a kind of novel we're part of? That's just as good, isn't it?"

He looks blank. Says nothing. Returns to his breakfast.

I feel even more beastly.

He's on edge this morning. Apart from the National Library, which opens for a half-day on Saturdays, every other library and archive closes at the end of today.

Despite the deadline, by the time we get out the door it's 9:45.

"Everything's already open!" my dad shrieks as we're leaving. His arm is already raised to hail a cab when we reach the main street. "Henrietta Street," he says before even closing the car door. "And we're in a bit of a hurry."

"Oh, well, in that case," the driver says, turning back to us and smiling. He pats his large belly. "I'll lean a wee bit to one side to allow some extra weight to flow into the right foot."

Like any ride that has the pressure of time attached, this one feels achingly slow, with stops, it seems, at every. single. light. Even with a heavy right foot, the cabbie seems to drive with the speed and motivation of a tour bus. *And on your right, you can see the headquarters of the Workers Union . . .*

"A mug o' tea, a pint o' Guinness, a slab o' cheese, and a thick slice o' soda bread. That's heaven now, isn't it?" the taxi driver asks, apropos of nothing, his face large and smiling in the rear-view mirror.

"Yes, yes," my dad replies, trying to chuckle and not doing a very good job. I lean forward and take over, chatting to the driver about the joys of Guinness, the pubs with the best pour, the kind of soda bread we had yesterday, the beer we're still hoping to try before we leave.

"And here on the left is Daniel O'Connell," the driver tells us, pointing to a tall bronze statue of a caped man, whose head is white with bird shit. "The Emancipator, he is. Campaigned long and hard for Catholic emancipation, he did. Seems good and right that he's bronzed for his troubles, isn't it?" He lifts his hand to the statue as we pass. "G'night, Dan," he says with a smirk in his voice.

Eventually — eventually — after what feels like the complete scenic tour of Dublin, we arrive at the bottom of Henrietta Street, where construction vehicles have blocked the entrance.

"You can just leave us here at the corner," my dad says, open-ing the cab door before it has come to a complete stop. He hands the driver a fold of euros, mutters thanks, and scurries towards the sidewalk.

Inside the Registry of Deeds, we exchange friendly greetings with the security guard whose Irish accent is so thick I do not understand a word that comes out of his mouth — not one — before signing in, locking up our coats and bags, and heading upstairs. My dad replied yes, yes to all of the security guard's questions, so as we are climbing the stairs to the library, I ask how he manages to understand him.

"Oh, I didn't understand a word," my dad replies. "I just didn't want to be contrary."

He pushes into the library and we begin assembling ourselves at a desk, when a woman on the other side of the room stands up and asks if I am Alison Wearing.

Maybe I should say: this sort of thing does not happen to me. In fact, quite the opposite: I am the doppelgänger of a famous local actor and singer, so I am constantly mistaken for her when I walk around our hometown of Stratford, Ontario, and regularly offered compliments on my (her) latest performance. I used to correct people, laugh with them at the resemblance — yes, I know, the spit-ting image! — but it's all rather time-consuming (and less funny the three hundredth time), so now I just smile and say thank you so much, you're very kind.

So while I am quite used to being recognized in public places, I'm not actually used to being recognized as myself.

The woman, Sharon, reminds me that we met during a literary festival on the Sunshine Coast of British Columbia last summer. She and her husband hosted a dinner at their seaside home for all of the authors. Which is downright eerie, because only a few weeks ago, I ran into the director of that same festival on a BC ferry — an extraordinary coincidence in itself — and after marvelling at *that* serendipity and chatting for a while, I asked her if she might be able to send me the contact information of the lovely couple who had hosted that dinner during the festival.

One half of whom now stands in front of me in the Registry of Deeds in Dublin.

It takes me a few seconds before I am able to do anything but stare and blink.

Sharon is here exploring her ancestry as well, though she's as flushed and relaxed as if she'd spent the week at the beach. She likes to do this for at least two weeks every year, she tells us, and enjoys spending every hour she can in this building, would set up a cot in the corner if she could. Doesn't even take a break for lunch.

My father is practically rapturous. He stops short of leaping over the desk physically, but in every other sense he catapults himself towards her. The two of them exchange animated descriptions of their missions, trading questions and abstruse suggestions about baronies and townlands and tithe applotments and poll ordinances and parish registries of Killaspugbrone and Kilmacshalgan and Knocknageeha. It's like watching the reunion of two people from a small exotic country conversing with ebullient relief in a language they haven't been able to speak for years.

As it is with these sorts of things, one minute it's improbably miraculous that I have run into Sharon from Sechelt, British Columbia, in the Registry of Deeds in Dublin — my dad takes a picture of us together next to all the dusty tomes — and the next minute it's the most natural thing in the world. *Can I borrow a pencil, Sharon? I'm not sure how to find that, Dad, let's go and ask Sharon*, et cetera.

Based on something that Sharon has told my father, he now thinks we should relocate every one of the entries we found the other day and review them to see if any of the persons mentioned in any of the deeds has the word *Esquire* after his name. Though I have no idea why this could possibly be worth the effort of climbing up and down the ladders and heaving dozens of thirty-pound tomes onto and off shelves and tables, or how this could possibly help him understand why his relatives left Ireland when they did, I do not ask *why*. That much, at least, I have learned over the last five days. I simply roll up my sleeves, gird my bum shoulder, and begin hoisting tombstones, hoping that that wrestler-cum-librarian might walk past from time to time and give me a hand.

He doesn't.

But Sharon does stand up at one point, blushing and laughing. In the middle of one of the eighteenth century registries she has been consulting, opposite a page of flowery calligraphy, is a full-page sketch. On the left is a drawing of a woman with long hair and the face of a bird. On the right is a man in a military uniform with a chest medal, epaulettes, and a line of large buttons running down the front of the jacket. The man has thick side burns, a twirling moustache, and a massive naked erection. He is giving the woman a kick and above him are penned the words, *How dare you say I married you*.

It is the very last thing one would expect to see in one of these sombre books, and I just love that it's been sitting there, uncensored, quietly shocking and/or entertaining genealogists for centuries.

As we are saying our farewell, Sharon invites me to come and work on my next book in her family's oceanfront guest cabin. It's completely private, she explains. The only stipulation is that they won't accept payment of any kind.

I am astounded by the kindness of the offer and my dad pats me on the shoulder, encouraging me to accept.

"You writers do get interesting offers," he says as we're heading back outside. "It must help take the sting out of the lack of income, security, stability, or possibility of retirement."

We are all the way down Henrietta Street before I can stop laughing.

We take another cab across town to the Manuscript Reading Room, where my dad dives right into a file that is waiting for him at the counter. It's just one small booklet, so he can handle it on his own, he explains. "And you have your friend . . ." he says, gesturing towards one of the men at the counter.

I turn to see Callum, who greets me with a smile and an outstretched hand. "When I noticed your father's order for materials, I knew you'd be back . . . and . . . em . . . I thought you might be interested in . . . em . . . having a gander at these." He reaches under the counter and hands me a stack of papers. It's a series of photocopied articles and webpages: *Washed Ashore: The Spanish Armada, Divers Recover Four Spanish Armada Cannons,* Wikipedia's lengthy entry for *Spanish Armada in Ireland.*

It's so sweet.

Callum blushes like a schoolboy when I thank him, shrugs excessively, and finds reason to brush something from the knee of his trousers before resuming his duties. "Have you been able to take in many of the sights of Dublin, then?" he asks after a moment.

I smile. "Well, we went to a play the other night."

"Oh, did you, now? What play was that, then?"

I open my mouth, hesitate. "It was . . . *Erect but Unstable.*"

Callum lurches backwards and laughs. "Erect but Unstable! That sounds like me at the end of every day!"

I smile. Leave it at that.

"Your father is a hard-working man," Callum says, looking over at my dad, who seems to be speed-reading, cramming, like a student trying to finish an exam before the bell rings. The sight breaks my heart.

This seems as good a time as any to confirm this definitively: my dad has not found any of the information he came to Dublin hoping to find.

I am quite prepared to take the blame for this, for everything — I've been a pathetic assistant, let's face it, deplorable: distracted and dismissive — but Callum leans over and tries to relieve some of my guilt.

"Your father doesn't give himself enough credit. He's an assiduous researcher, first-class. He mentioned that he was here a decade ago on a similar mission, and he seems to think he didn't do a thorough enough job then, but I've tried to assure him that it's not for lack of talent or dedication that he finds himself empty-handed. The materials he's searching for simply fail to exist, it pains me to say."

"Yes, we've heard that from a number of people. It's just that my father is very determined . . ."

"As he should rightly be!" Callum whispers, bouncing his fist on the desk for quiet emphasis. "But there comes a point in these sorts of projects when one must surrender to the great unknown . . ." he says, turning his palm to the air, softening his gaze, his tone — ". . . to turn, perhaps, to the larger stories of history and employ the faculties of imagination . . ."

Callum moves to help someone at the counter and I look over at my dad again. His head is bobbing, his arm juddering. I watch the strange disease from afar, the way it jerks at him, how distracting and frustrating it must be, how terrifying. Yet how gracefully he deals with it all. The way he accepts what is, and goes on.

I want to be like that, I realize as I watch him.

I want to be someone who accepts what life serves and carries on without complaint, someone who is forever reaching for the next taste of joy. I want to be someone so filled with curiosity and determination that I trundle around foreign cities looking for obscure pieces of a puzzle that might help me understand who I am, and still be game for Zumba when I'm eighty. I want to giggle and scurry and speak only well of people, to sing in a Mennonite choir, take an erotic massage course, celebrate nothing in particular, and Just Let Things Go. I want to lack self-consciousness, to care passionately about all manner of things, to devote myself, to be curious and open-minded, to listen and nod, laugh at every opportunity, and to have all the time in the world for love.

Perhaps this is what a legacy truly is.

∽

My dad closes the folder he's been looking at, stands up quickly, and scurries towards me. Callum strides over to assist him. "I was just telling your daughter what a fine researcher you are, sir," he says, welcoming the documents and smiling. "And that you should think well of your efforts." Then he turns to me and nods. "As well as the efforts of your daughter, of course."

My dad thanks him, straightens his papers. Looks frazzled.

"As a matter of fact," Callum continues, "we were just discussing the need, at certain points in this sort of endeavour, to step away from the documentation and allow ourselves to be informed by other types of information, the larger stories, as it were."

My dad nods hastily and consults his watch.

Callum goes on. "If we consider the living conditions of the vast majority of Irishmen at the time, sir, the level of privation and servitude, and the dearth of opportunity for advancement or the improvement of condition, it's not difficult to imagine how a man might dream of greater possibility on distant shores."

"And then there's the weather," I add facetiously.

"Indeed!" Callum agrees. "But you both have the very good fortune of being in Dublin during a heat wave! They're calling for Mediterranean temperatures right through the weekend: sixteen degrees today and eighteen tomorrow!"

My dad flashes me a quick grin. We all shake hands and say our goodbyes.

"Eighteen degrees!" my dad says once we're out in the hallway. He presses the button for the elevator. "I should have brought my Speedo!"

Outside the library, my dad spots a poster for a choral concert tomorrow night.

"Oh, look, they're going to be singing *Zadok the Priest*," he says, moving closer to see the details. "Do you know that piece? It's one of Handel's coronation anthems. It's got a terrific opening." He thrusts his arm forward and sings, "ZAAADOK THE PRIEEEEEST!" in the deepest and loudest baritone he can muster. Every person on the sidewalk glances over, even those on the opposite side of the road, but my dad has never noticed or been dissuaded by the attention of passers-by. While he belts out the next line — "AAAND NAAATHAN THE PRO-PHET" — I scribble down the concert details, then tip to the back of my notebook and scrawl *His Complete Lack of Self-Consciousness — Even on Crowded Streets*.

Which reminds me of his complete lack of self-consciousness, even while dancing.

Which reminds me.

Move 4 Parkinson's is starting in just over an hour.

"So, that dance thing is st—"

"We still need to go to the Representative Church Body Library," my dad says, putting up his umbrella. "It's in Braemor Park."

"Oh . . . I didn't realize there was still . . . It's just that the dance thing is starting in an hour."

"We'll have to take a bus," he says, ignoring my comment and walking ahead. "It leaves from Dame Street, on the other side of the Liffey, so we'll need to walk quickly."

I press my lips together, flutter my eyes. "So, what is it we're looking for . . . there?"

He doesn't answer. Or isn't listening. I'm not sure which. And I understand that it's completely ridiculous to want to go dancing. But I really need to do this. I need to dance with my dad in Dublin. It's just too beautiful a thing to do together, too romantic a way to cap this father-daughter adventure, too perfect an image to carry, story to treasure, moment to capture. But it's not going to happen. Nothing is going to happen. In one week together, nothing has happened: no great discovery, no big moment, nothing important or significant at all. Nor is that likely to change. Because we need to go and look for a parish record, a marriage settlement, some kind of a document, which, we've been told several times, probably doesn't exist at all, and, if it did, would only help to establish, perhaps, whether or not my gr-gr-gr-gr-grandfather (?) had title to a largish piece of land, a smallish piece of land, or, perhaps — stop the presses! — farmed someone else's land.

So rather than spending an hour dancing together in Dublin — I could not conjure a grander Life Moment for my mental archive if I tried — we are heading to the Representative Church Body Library, a name that makes my own body ache with every expression of divine feminine wisdom and spirituality that has been repressed or burned at the stake over the last two thousand years.

I'm trying to buck up, suck it up, grow up, do a whole repertoire of up things, but it's not working. I'm so disappointed, I'm on the verge of tears. It makes no rational sense, but it takes everything I've got to hold myself together.

We walk in silence to Dame Street, where we wait, trying, along with the rest of Dublin, to ignore the fact that it is pouring rain. After the tenth or eleventh bus wearing the wrong number sloshes by us, I ask the man next to me for help. We're looking for the number fourteen bus going to Braemor Park.

"You're grand," he tells us. "It's de buses're arseways."

I turn to my father. "I think it's coming."

"Tourists, are you?" another man asks. "I hope to go to America." I make the hurried correction.

"Oh, Canada, so it is." He nods. Considers. "Cold but sane," he concludes.

A description I find I have no argument with.

The man is friendly, quick to smile. Asks what we've been able to see of Ireland thus far and I reply, "VERY LITTLE," before my father takes over, recounting cheerful tales of our genealogical adventures until I am drooping with guilt.

We should be sure to get out of Dublin a bit, the man advises us, see the countryside. "The walk from Greystones to Bray, for example. Or the harbour at Howth. I'm from County Galway, myself, so I cannot help but recommend the Cliffs of Moher. Everyone goes there to do the deed, of course, it's become the suicide capital of Ireland, but oh, it's grand. Lovely place, if you like the outdoors."

Both my father and I appear to have been struck dumb.

"There was a boom awhile back," the man continues, unperturbed by our silence. "Actually, it was more like an *illuuuuusion*." He draws the word out for emphasis. "And the wealth of the average Irishman *quadruuuuupled* in the space of ten or fifteen years. First time in history, Ireland began importing people instead of exporting them like we've done for centuries." He smiles, enjoying the accomplishment for a moment. "Well, o' course, it all crashed. And then, well, the Cliffs of Moher became a busy place, I'm sorry to say." He tips his umbrella and leans out to get a good look at the next bus. "And here's yours, the number fourteen! Don't be buying your father a ticket, now. Those who've lived to such a grand age do their Dublin bus travel for free."

"I might be insulted by that," my dad says as we step onto the bus and he proceeds without paying, "but it was so sweetly meant." And

it was. By the time I pay my fare and grab onto a handgrip, I've
pulled out of my dance doldrums.

A boy in a tweed cap gives up his seat and my dad thanks him
and sits down. Then he looks up at me and shouts as if I were at
the other end of the bus. "THE WHOLE TIME THAT FELLOW
WAS SPEAKING, I KEPT THINKING OF THAT FAMOUS
QUOTE OF YEATS'S: *BEING IRISH, HE HAD AN ABIDING SENSE
OF TRAGEDY, WHICH SUSTAINED HIM THROUGH TEMPORARY
PERIODS OF JOY.*"

I pull out my notebook and begin to jot down the quote as the
bus lurches forward.

"*. . . an abiding sense of tragedy* . . . And what's the next bit?"

"WHICH SUSTAINED HIM . . ." my dad repeats.

"*. . . which sustained him . . .*"

". . . THROUGH TEMPORARY PERIODS OF JOY."

An older woman sitting beside my father leans towards him.

"Aren't they lovely, sir, those periods of joy?" She lets laughter
bubble through her voice. "I had one just today."

"Oh . . . well, it's Yeats," my dad says in response.

The woman nods. "Is it, now? Yeats. Well, he'll brook no argument from me. We all need our periods of joy. Even the temporary
ones are welcome." She turns and looks out the window of the bus,
her face drained of laughter again.

My dad turns to me. "I hope you jotted that down too," he says
quietly, flashing me a playful smile.

Gradually the neighbourhoods become leafier, the houses set
back behind front gardens and trees, space and privacy. It's wonderful to be getting out of the city centre and I've climbed out of my
tetchy state enough to enjoy the ride, the views, the glimpse into
another side of Dublin, the faces of the people on the bus, the lives
I begin to imagine for each of them, when Braemor Park is called.

∾

The Representative Church Body Library looks like a prison, albeit a small one with minimal security. We are buzzed in by a man who seems not to know anything about the joy the Irish are entitled to.

Inside, we are greeted by bland walls, the reek of piety, and a sign telling us to stow our belongings in the lockers provided before proceeding upstairs to the library. My dad pulls out his notebook and pencil, and I put on a thick application of tinted lip gloss before stuffing my backpack in the locker, only because it is the most heretical act I can conjure in that moment.

The entire staircase is lined with portraits of dour, etiolated priests. "This looks fun," I mumble as I climb. And I can feel myself sweating involuntarily, as I used to do when forced to attend church, manufacturing an overabundance of sinfully feminine pheromones as we approach the office. There is a man waiting for us at the top of the stairs. I have noticed him without looking at him, a peripheral awareness, and the very last thing in the world I am expecting him to be is . . . well, there is only one word for it: hot.

He is *hot*.

Youngish — early forties? — radiant, with a broad chest, a kind face, and thick, longish, curly blond hair. He looks as if he's just jogged in from the rugby pitch, and he also looks sweet, with an endearing smile and a generosity in his gestures, an innate grace.

What a fine Representative of the Church Body, I think to myself, wondering if that same phrase has just gone through my father's mind as well.

"Welcome," the man says. "How can I be of service?"

As my father and I race to answer, I take note of how invested I am, all of a sudden, in establishing whether or not my gr-gr-gr-gr-grandfather (?) had title to land or farmed someone else's land. The hot man   Eamon — touches the stubble on his chin as he listens to us ramble on, cracking the smallest and sexiest of smiles before guiding us into the office of a man who is contrasting in every way: terminally penitent with large, yellowing teeth, projectile bad breath, and decades of not enough showering.

Eamon explains our search to the Holy Man of Halitosis and expresses concerns about the dates of the documents we seek before disappearing and taking every ounce of my enthusiasm about this endeavour with him. HMH talks to us about the difficulty of locating documents with a seriousness that makes me want to leap out the window. The office doesn't smell, only because the air hasn't been stirred up enough in the last fifty years to be capable of carrying odour, but there is a heavy sourness about the place. From every wall, a man's sanctimonious face stares down, silently condemning the concept of pleasure.

"I have to pee," I announce before quickly rephrasing, "Sorry, is there a . . . public restroom?"

HMH looks down, off to the left. "You'll find the toilets on the lower level," he says, softly disgusted. And all the way down the stairs I wish, wish, wish I'd had the foresight to carry a small bottle of whiskey in my backpack on these research adventures. Why on earth didn't I think of that until now?

On my way back up the stairs, I take a moment to examine the portraits of priests, bishops, and cardinals that line the stairs, to stare into the eyes of these men and try to see them, understand what lies behind the expressions on their faces, their dogged and untiring disapproval.

I get nowhere. Because the portraits are all flat. Replication rather than art. The depictions might be faithful, but they're empty.

The American portrait artist John Singer Sargent described a portrait as being *a painting in which something is wrong with the mouth*. Which is something that has always fascinated me about portraiture: that its finest and most successful examples, the portraits that allow for the spirit of the subject to lift into existence in unexpected, even uncanny, ways are often those in which the details are inaccurate.

Chagall claimed that *one cannot be precise and still be true*; Picasso famously defined art as *the lie that helps us realize the truth*; Van Gogh's aim was *to make those very incorrectnesses, those deviations, remodellings, changes in reality, so that they may become, yes, lies if you like — but truer than the literal truth*; and then yesterday there was Oscar Wilde: *Lying, the telling of beautiful untrue things, is the proper aim of art.*

All of which has me returning, yet again, to the question of truth. What and where is it, and what does it mean?

I do not have the answer to that question at the moment. But I do know that it is not to be found in the stairwell of the Representative Church Body Library.

I return to the office and find HMH alone at his desk. "You'll find your father in the library," he says, not looking up and pointing with the end of his pencil.

On my way down the narrow hallway, I lift a pamphlet entitled "Pastoral Care of Homosexual Persons" and fold it into my back pocket.

My dad shakes his head when he sees me. "It doesn't sound very promising," he says, "but they've gone to have a look, anyway." Then, no doubt sensing my claustrophobia, "We'll probably be on our way shortly."

The library is a small, unremarkable room lined with metal bookcases. For want of anything else to do, I scan the shelves: *Ethics Matters, The Ethics of Jesus, Market Complicity and Human Ethics, The Ethics of Human Cloning* . . . and then I am astonished to have my finger catch on a familiar name: Murdoch. *The Sovereignty of Good: Studies in Ethics and the Philosophy of Religion.*

I tip it off the shelf. Open it at random. Instantly spy two relevant sentences.

"Hey, Dad, remember our conversation the other night in the pub about transcendence?"

He nods.

"Well, listen to this. *Transcendence leads us not to some abstract spiritual realm but into a reality of here and now which selfishness normally conceals. Moral development, and also the experience of art and beauty, are the penetration of this veil.*"

"The experience of art, beauty, *and birds*," he corrects. "They forgot birds."

"She, actually," I close the book and show him the cover. "It's Iris Murdoch."

He looks surprised. "Oh, read it again," he suggests. So I do.

His face is strained. Every muscle seems to be flexed. "What do you suppose she means by *selfishness normally conceals . . . ?*"

"I guess that when we are so focused on ourselves, our own thoughts and petty lives, we can't experience transcendence, but that through art and beauty and moral development, *and birds*, we can."

"Yes, I suppose. Though I'm not sure what she means about transcendence leading us into a reality of the here and now," he says. "I thought the whole point of transcendence was that you got out of that."

"Well, no, isn't that the great paradox?"

He creases his face still further. "Isn't *what* the great paradox?"

"That there's no abstract spiritual realm, as she says. Buddhists say the same thing: it's all just here, now. Shangri-La, paradise, utopia: there're actually all just here, wherever you are now. It's a mental state, not a physical place. The more fully present we are in this moment, the closer we are."

"To what?" He seems annoyed.

"To transcendence, to the sacred, to God, if you want to call it that. I mean, isn't that what we've been talking about, Dad, with the opera and the birding and so on? Whatever transcendence might come of them is all the result of focus, being fully presen—"

"Well, no, I think . . ." He tries to cut me off mid-sentence. He has been cutting me off mid-sentence for much of my life.

"Wait, wait," I continue. "Just listen. Aren't they all just different expressions of the same kind of surrender, to beauty, to mystery, to ecstasy, to the present moment, the here and n—"

"But that's the bit that seems overly simpli . . ." He starts to cut me off again and stops.

I am not yet able to appreciate the humour in our having a tiff, the first real squabble we've had in seven full days of being together, about, of all things, transcendence, in, of all places, the Representative Church Body Library. What I do find funny is that the next time I glance over at the doorway, Eamon is standing there, leaning against the door frame looking as sexy and relaxed as it is possible to appear in this particular setting.

He's terribly sorry to interrupt. As he suspected, the records we are searching for were among those destroyed in the Four Courts fire. He knows how disappointing that can be, and again, he's terribly sorry. He wishes us the best of luck with our search and hopes we have a very pleasant stay in Dublin.

My dad thanks him. Excessively.

Eamon smiles. Strides back down the hallway.

"Shall we ask him if he wants to have dinner with us?" I suggest softly, though not as softly as my father might have liked. He waves at me to be quiet. Then laughs and whispers, "Actually, I'd already thought of that."

I take my phone out of my back pocket and take a picture of the Murdoch quote before we saunter down the pallid procession of portraits and back out into the fresh, wild air.

∾

My dad looks at his watch when we step outside. "Oh, I guess we could have gone to the dancing after all," he says with apology in his voice.

"That's okay, Dad. We can go dancing another time. I'm sure there's a group in Toronto, if you want . . ."

"Oh, do you think so? Well, that might be intriguing... although I think I'd rather dance with someone like that Eamon fellow," he says, pointing back towards the library. "And a Parkinson's group might not have that . . . sort of thing."

We both laugh. Then he looks at the ground, becomes serious. "And I wasn't sure what kind of shape the other people were going to be in."

The admission is a hard boot to my chest.

It hadn't occurred to me. That far from being a glorious moment, it might have been excruciating: a room full of people at far more advanced stages of this illness, a glimpse of something neither of us wants or needs to see. The whole idea suddenly seems insensitive, painfully, stupidly selfish. The same goes for all my childish antics this week, my adolescent pouting and resistance in libraries. It's as if I've been looking for some perverse way to wrest time, to lock it in my fingers, slow it down. To keep feeling like a child so I do not have to grow up and face something I do not want to see. That I am losing my father. That I will lose my father. And that it is time to grow up. To let go of the twelve-year-old girl who lost her father to a truer way of life and become the adult woman who might some-day need to take care of him.

By the time we reach the bus stop, it has stopped raining, and we are on an empty, open road. We stand together in a suburb of South Dublin and wait. Share silence. Listen to all the birds we have not been able to hear in the city. Delicate blossoms against our ears.

I look up at a feathering of clouds, filaments of visual song. And then I look at my father beside me. The way he stands and observes it all.

His cap covers most of his thinning white hair. His jaw trembles, as if held by a loosening hinge, and his left arm quivers at his side. The sight fills me with ferocious love.

We stand together. At a bus stop. Under quiet and cloud.

It is a perfectly unremarkable moment.

And all that is important and true is here.

SATURDAY

SEOMRA NA LÉITHEOIEACHTA

We're back where we started. The elegantly carved desks and chairs, the natural light billowing and sighing from the vast dome, the creaking wooden floors. There is nothing urgent to be found here today, apparently. My dad wants to leaf through a few files that were on his *if there's time* list, while he has the chance. He doesn't need my help with anything, "but just having you here beside me is wonderful," he says with a wrinkle in his voice.

So I'm sitting at his side, wrapping my arms around this moment, its poignant, joyful song.

We will never do anything like this again. I may never have the privilege of spending so much carefree time with my dad as I have just now, scurrying around Dublin, father and daughter on a lark. And it is so obvious, yet just as easily forgotten, that this time we have — with our parents, our children, the people we love — is so very finite, so very fleeting, so very, very small.

~ා

A bell rings.

Followed by a woman's soft voice.

The library will be closing in five minutes.

My dad is buried in papers. He has his left hand tucked behind his back and the tremor is fierce at the moment, begging for his attention, like an invisible, insatiable child. I watch with tear-sparkled eyes, wishing I could spare him all of this, save him.

But I cannot, of course. Any more than I can hang on to time.

I can only be here with him. Offer him my devotion, my love. And be glad of this simple moment together.

"Well, I guess that's it," my dad says and closes the file. Sighs. Then he turns to me, and his face opens into the warmest of smiles. "You're free."

ACKNOWLEDGMENTS

This story first danced into being on my porch one afternoon, shortly after I returned from Ireland. I thought it might make a nice short essay, something I could toss off by the end of the summer. When I still hadn't gotten us to a single library by page ten, however, I knew I had something larger on my hands.

Fortunately, I was beginning an appointment as Writer-in-Residence that fall, and I am tremendously grateful to Catherine Bush and the Guelph-Humber MFA Program, the University of Guelph's School of English and Theatre Studies, as well as the Canada Council for the Arts, for providing the space, time and means to focus on this project.

From there, I was lucky enough to work in a sun-drenched office at the Performing Arts Lodge in Stratford, Ontario, and I thank the board and residents of PAL for that privilege, as well as the Ontario Arts Council, whose financial support helped me to put down a few of the balls I must normally keep in the air. It is always easier to write when we do not also have to juggle.

With the deepest possible humility, I thank the Anishinaabe and Haudenosaunee peoples upon whose ancestral territories the towns of Guelph and Stratford, Ontario, now sit. And I bow my head to the Cree, Métis and Anishinaabe peoples of the territories surrounding what became known as Chapleau, Ontario, with most profound regret and respect.

Samantha Albert read early drafts and helped me to understand the true heart of the story, and I am blessed to have such a patient and insightful first reader and friend.

My agent, Martha Webb, is a dream I hope never to wake up from. I owe her a thousand thanks for honest support, acumen, and faith, as well as to dear Deirdre Molina, who was beyond generous in offering her help with, and belief in, this manuscript during its first steps out into the world.

Great gratitude to my editor, Susan Renouf, for being willing to get behind this book, and for gently showing me what it needed to take flight. I am delighted and honoured to be published by ECW Press, and offer my deepest thanks to David Caron, Susannah Ames, Jessica Albert, Laura Pastore, and the entire team of dedicated enthusiasts at ECW.

The final draft of this book was written while I was Writer-in-Residence at the paradise that is Green College, University of British Columbia, in Vancouver, on the traditional, ancestral, and unceded territory of the Musqueam people. There was so much about that residency and those surroundings that nourished the manuscript's critical final iteration, but many sessions of ocean counsel, some glittering conversations with Mark Vessey, and one in particular about trusting the truth in art, were especially helpful.

Ruth Strunz was kind enough to comb through the manuscript to ensure that my renditions of Dubliners and their dialogues were accurate, and she leapt in again to help me with the pronunciation of place names and Irish words for the audiobook version. Stratford Festival voice and dialect coach Nancy Benjamin also graciously helped with the Dublin accents and dialects. Any remaining infelicities in that recording or in this text, however, are my responsibility entirely.

I must also acknowledge James Joyce, for his *Dubliners* characters came to life for me so vividly all over that city that I've given several of them cameo appearances, though obviously they didn't exist to anyone but me. None of them does or says anything particularly notable, but I enjoyed the spectral dimension they added, and it makes for a nice treasure hunt if you're into that sort of thing.

Lastly, I wish to offer my gratitude to my family—all of you— but especially to this trinity of gentle men: Jarmo Jalava, Noah Jalava, and Dad.

ALISON WEARING is the bestselling author of
Confessions of a Fairy's Daughter, an Indigo
Top 50 Pick shortlisted for the Edna Staebler
Prize and longlisted for the RBC Taylor Prize,
and *Honeymoon in Purdah: An Iranian Journey*.
She leads writing workshops internationally
and online, and is also an award-winning
performer of original solo plays.